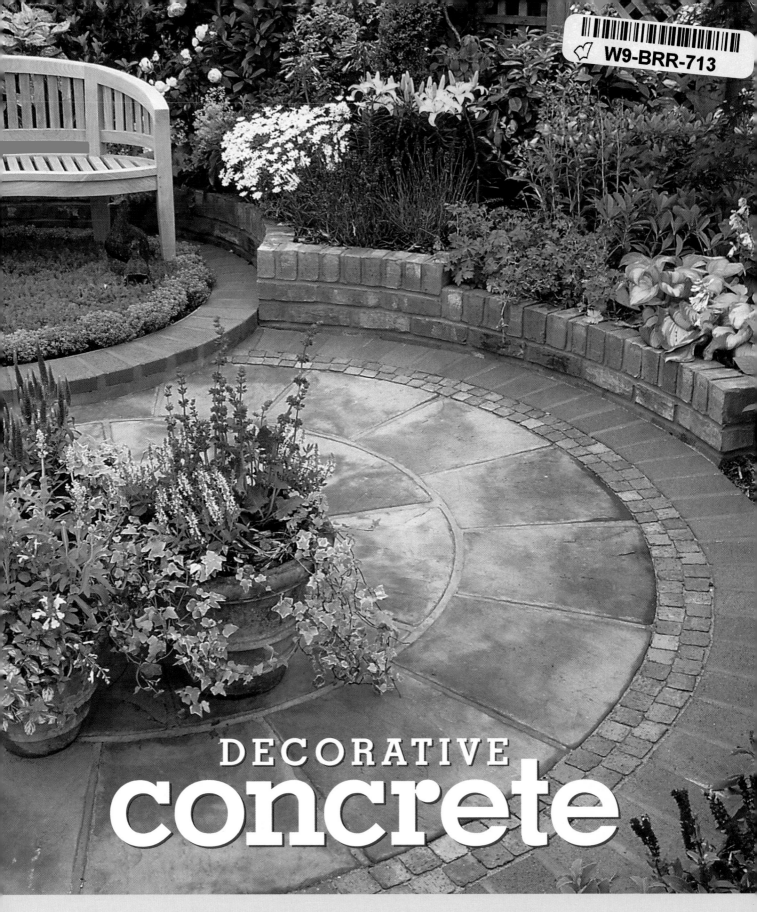

DECORATIVE
concrete

By Jeanne Huber and the Editors of Sunset Books

MENLO PARK · CALIFORNIA

Sunset Books

Vice President, General Manager: Richard A. Smeby
Vice President, Editorial Director: Bob Doyle
Production Director: Lory Day
Director of Operations: Rosann Sutherland
Marketing Manager: Linda Barker
Art Director: Vasken Guiragossian
Special Sales: Brad Mose

Staff for this book:

Developmental Editor: Linda J. Selden
Copy Editor: Carol Whiteley
Photo Editor: Carrie Dodson Davis
Art Director: Nina Bookbinder
Illustrator: Beverley Bozarth Colgan
Principal Photographer: Chuck Kuhn
Prepress Coordinator: Danielle Javier
Proofreader: Mary Roybal
Indexer: Phyllis Elving

For additional copies of Decorative Concrete *or any other Sunset book, call 1-800-526-5111 or visit us at www.sunset.com.*

Cover main image: interior design by Eugenia Erskine Jesberg; photography by E. Andrew McKinney. Bottom left: photography by Tim Street-Porter. Bottom middle: photography by Sonoma Cast Stone. Bottom right: photography by Sonoma Cast Stone. Cover design by Vasken Guiragossian.

A decorative material

Given the explosion of interest in using decorative concrete indoors and out, we are pleased to present this guide. In these pages, you will find a primer on the materials that go into decorative concrete as well as various techniques for shaping this highly versatile material. Professionals who work with decorative concrete use many specialty products and tools. We have tried to note those, but also to show how you can build projects on your own using materials that are more commonly available.

You will find scores of pictures of completed projects that you can use as design inspiration for your own projects or as a starting point for projects that you might want a professional to tackle. We've also included an array of projects that you might want to undertake on your own.

Many individuals and firms were expert resources for us in preparing this book. Among the professionals who aided us we are particularly thankful to Margaret Gibbs, Ted Bowman of Fred Hill Materials, Buddy Rhodes of Buddy Rhodes Studio, Cameron Nichols of Nichols Bros. Stoneworks, Pat Nordquist of Artisans Concrete Supply, Tommy Cook of Cook's Custom Creations, Steven Rosenblat of Sonoma Cast Stone, Nick Nicholson of Quikrete, and Rick Cash of R&A Concrete.

We could not have built the projects in this book without the assistance of Sheila Abrahams; Caulkins Alailima; Jane, David, and Kaza Ansley; Becky, Allison, Evan, and Andrew Beemer; Diane Bonciolini; Cedric Delobelle; Mihai Harangus; Lisa Splendid Jacklich of Napa Valley Artworks; Robyn Krutch; Terry Magill; Valerie Parker; Bob Stanton; and Penny Wisegram. Chuck Kuhn, the principal photographer for the book, also hauled his share of heavy materials and coped ably and in good humor with the fickle nature of hardening concrete.

Contents

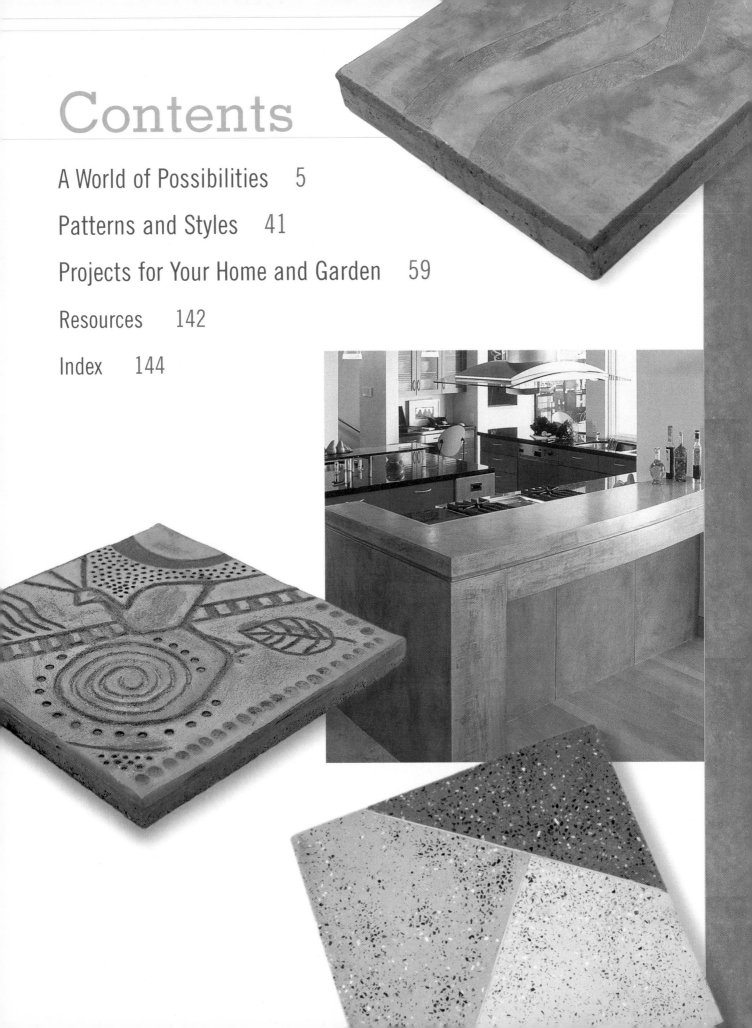

A world of possibilities

Inexpensive and strong, concrete holds up houses, paves driveways, and keeps fence posts from tipping over. But beyond these utilitarian roles, it also excels as a decorative material. Adding color, using special sand or gravel, and varying the surface finish change its look in nearly limitless ways. You can pour concrete into forms, sculpt it almost as if it were clay, and carve it after it is set but not yet very hard. No wonder decorative concrete is showing up in more and more houses in everything from countertops and fireplace surrounds to tabletops and garden art. Whether you tackle a project on your own or hire someone to do it, this chapter gives you the background you need to wind up with a great result.

Pick your style

WHETEVER THE STYLE OF YOUR HOME, you can use decorative concrete to good advantage. Indoor possibilities include countertops, sinks, fireplace surrounds, hearths, floors, and even furniture. For example, a dining room or sunroom table made of concrete can look gorgeous. Outdoors, you can use it to pave a path, embellish a dull driveway, or build big pots to hold flowers or even small trees. The possibilities are truly amazing.

Even in standard gray, concrete pairs beautifully with a wide array of materials. In the kitchen below, it partners with basketry, maple, stainless steel, tarnished steel (on drawer fronts), steel cabinet pulls, and even aspen branches, still with bark. See page 15 for details on how to create this type of concrete edge.

Concrete tiles tinted in varying shades suit this entry for a European country home. Cast into pillow-shaped forms, they have a rustic, hand-crafted look that would be equally at home in an adobe-style house.

Particularly with built-in elements such as countertops and fireplace surrounds, you'll want to tailor your projects to the style of your house. Intricate moldings work in a Victorian. In a Craftsman-style home, simpler shapes look best, although you can add carved or molded designs typical of the period if you wish. In a contemporary house, you might choose crisp edges and massive shapes.

Inset tiles featuring two small rabbits enliven an otherwise simple concrete fireplace surround, in a style that suits Craftsman and other traditional homes.

Cast concrete tinted olive gray serves as a focal point in a contemporary family room; the concrete hearth extends the width of the room and serves as a window seat along the wall to the right.

Concrete tiles with veins of contrasting color hint of marble and give this room an Asian look, especially when set off by an airy flower arrangement.

Mitered corners help this fireplace surround focus attention on the fire, similar to the way a picture frame sets off artwork. The clean lines of the surround also help establish a crisp, modern tone for the room.

Wavy-edged sinks, built-in drainboards, and other special features are all possible when made of concrete. This sink-and-countertop unit was cast upside down in a mold made with all the features in reverse.

This simple blue countertop owes much to its sinuous curve. Besides adding beauty, the edge creates enough space for multiple stools in this breakfast area. The curve also cuts down on the size of the countertop, keeping it from blocking access between the family room and the kitchen.

Pros and cons of decorative concrete

CONCRETE IS STRONG, READILY available, and relatively inexpensive. As a decorative material, it's also incredibly versatile:

❖ It's easy to customize, so you can get the color, size, and shape you want in a sink or fireplace surround.

❖ It can be mixed where you need it from materials you can carry in manageable loads. For example, you can build massive steps up a hillside without using heavy equipment.

❖ It stiffens on its own. You can use it to make tiles, pots, and other claylike projects, but you don't need a kiln.

❖ If you time it right, decorative concrete can be carved with little effort and no dust. You can make objects that look like carved stone using only a kitchen knife.

As with any material, there are also some downsides. Concrete is porous, so it stains. Outdoors, it may crack as it freezes and thaws. (See page 33 for ways to minimize these problems.) It's also prone to cracking when cast into certain shapes, and the top surface can wear noticeably. In addition, concrete is heavy: about 140 pounds per cubic foot. In an older house, you may need to strengthen the floor supports if you add thick countertops in the center of a room.

DOING IT YOURSELF VS. HIRING A PRO

Building with concrete on your own can be fun. But if a mix begins to harden before it's shaped, the project becomes a nightmare. If you're a novice, you may want to focus on garden projects and hire a pro for big indoor pieces. If you do tackle a countertop or other large project, practice on smaller pieces. Get help. And design poured-in-place projects so they can be removed if necessary (see page 20).

Heavy machinery would be needed to place boulders like these. But a home-owner built these steps himself from concrete he mixed in batches in a wheelbarrow and shaped by hand. He scattered pigments onto the surface and troweled them in, giving a variegated appearance similar to native stone in the area.

Tip

REMEMBER THAT you will need to move precast projects into place. If the weight scares you, consider doing as some concrete specialists do: hire piano movers.

9

Understanding the basic ingredients

MANY PEOPLE USE THE TERMS "cement" and "concrete" interchangeably, but the two materials are not the same. Cement is just glue. Concrete is what you get by mixing cement with aggregate (usually small rocks and sand) and enough water to produce a workable consistency. Some mixes also incorporate fibers, acrylic fortifiers, and other additives.

WATER

It may seem strange to look at water first, but this ingredient is actually the key to how your project turns out. Water makes concrete easy to shape, and sets off a chemical reaction known as hydration that causes the cement to harden.

Incorporating just the right amount of water is crucial. If you use too little, you'll wind up with a mix that's hard to form and trowel smooth. You may find air gaps along edges when you remove forms. If you add too much water,

6% AIR

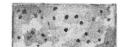
11% PORTLAND CEMENT

41% GRAVEL OR CRUSHED STONE (COARSE AGGREGATE)

26% SAND (FINE AGGREGATE)

16% WATER

Although it's the key to holding everything together, cement accounts for the least bulk of all the major ingredients in concrete. There are many recipes for concrete, so proportions vary.

Tip

TO MAKE CONCRETE flow well with less water, substitute acrylic or latex fortifier (also sold as "bonding adhesive") for up to half the usual water. However, do not use fortifier with bagged mixes that specify adding only water.

however, your project will become weak and prone to cracking. The excess water goes to the surface as you shape the concrete, creating tiny tunnels that remain when the mix hardens. The tunnels make concrete porous, the characteristic that leads to staining and frost damage.

Ironically, once cement stiffens, abundant moisture is good. It allows hydration to continue, so the concrete becomes even harder and more crack resistant. Once the concrete dries, however, hydration ceases. Adding water after that point won't restart the process.

To get your mix just right:

❖ Add just enough water when combining ingredients to make the concrete workable.

❖ Handle the mix as little as possible. Place it close to where you need it. Level it quickly. Delay troweling until surface water disappears.

❖ Keep the concrete damp for at least several days, up to a month if possible.

TYPES OF CEMENT

The most common cement, known as Portland cement, comes in many different types. But if you buy a bagged mix, you won't necessarily know which kind of cement it contains. Use other characteristics, such as suitable thickness or speed of setting, to select the best type for your project. If you create your own concrete mix, you can use the standard cement that's sold in bags at building-materials stores, which may be labeled Type I (general purpose) or Type I-II (similar, but more resistant to breaking down).

If you develop your skills and become interested in casting intricate shapes, you may also want to incorporate small amounts of specialty cements, such as fly ash or metakaolin. Known as pozzolans these fine powders act like miniature BBs, helping other ingredients slip into place with less water. This results in a denser, stronger concrete that gives you the ability to produce crisp details. Buy these cements at specialty companies (see Resources, page 142). They are incorporated in some bagged mixes.

White or gray?

Standard Portland cement is gray. White cement is also available, although at a higher price, from masonry-supply companies and concrete ready-mix firms (see Resources, page 142). White cement is worth searching for if you want to add pigments to produce bright colors.

Tinting gray cement produces muted colors.

If you use white cement, you may also want to use white aggregate, such as crushed limestone (dolomite or calcite) or quartzite sands. If you use an additive cement, choose metakaolin, which is often dark.

Tip

If you get concrete on your hands, wash it off promptly. Follow up with vinegar at the end of the day. An acid, vinegar counteracts the alkalinity of cement and keeps your skin from chafing.

Safety

Cement is dusty when dry and caustic when damp, and cement mixtures often contain considerable quantities of crystalline silica, which can damage your lungs. You may need to wear a disposable respirator (the two-elastic kind) when you work with dry ingredients. Always wear rubber gloves, and add boots if needed. Check the top of your gloves and boots frequently for unnoticed spills that may cause blisters you won't feel at first.

Concrete made with white cement, not the usual gray, produces vibrant color like that in this bathroom. Concrete tiles on the walls, the steps, and the base of the tub surround were custom-colored to complement marble around the top of the tub and the tumbled marble tiles on the floor.

AGGREGATE

Sand and gravel play two roles in the projects presented in this book: structural and decorative.

From a structural standpoint, sand and especially gravel are what give concrete its strength. They, not cement, should account for most of the volume. A range of particle sizes works best because it allows small pieces to fit in between big ones. Use sharp-edged aggregate (crushed or blasted) if you have a choice, since it packs tighter than rounded beach sand or river rock. Look for mason's sand or all-purpose sand. Avoid play sand, which has round grains of fairly uniform size.

The biggest particles should not exceed one-fifth the thickness of your project. For thin projects, you might need particles no more than $1/8$ inch or even less. But paths, floors, and thick areas such as hearths benefit from larger gravel. Go up to $3/4$ inch for a 4-inch slab. With bagged mixes, the depth limits on the label indicate maximum aggregate size. Concrete sold for slabs more than 2 inches thick contains gravel up to $1/2$ inch across. Sand mixes designed for $1/16$-inch applications use finer grit than those for $1/2$-inch layers.

Using glass aggregate

You may be tempted to use broken glass for some or all of the aggregate. However, researchers who study industrial uses of concrete have found that some glass reacts with the alkaline content of cement when moisture is present for long periods. An expansive gel forms at the glass edges, cracking the concrete or ejecting some of the surface glass. In a dam this phenomenon is a critical issue. In decorative projects, however, it's less of a problem. For outdoor projects, take the precaution of replacing part of the mix water with acrylic or latex fortifier and consider switching to white cement, which has a low alkaline content. Indoors, there is no concern except for use on a shower floor or a sink.

Concrete usually winds up with a thin film of cement and fine sand at the surface. But grinding and then polishing wear that away and reveal the aggregate underneath. On this fireplace surround, the result is the sparkle of fragments of yellow traffic lights. A steel I-beam serves as a mantle.

Like confetti, bits of colored glass suspended in white concrete give this countertop its distinctive look.

Buying decorative aggregate

There are two basic ways to decorate concrete with aggregate: scatter it on the surface or polish the concrete to reveal what's mixed into the interior. Specialty companies (see Resources, page 142) sell sand and gravel sorted by color and size. Ask for recommendations about types that won't react with cement and cause the concrete to break down.

Specify "one-fourth minus" to get a range of sand and gravel sizes up to ¼-inch diameter. Ask for "one-fourth neat" to get gravel all about ¼ inch in diameter. You might ask for a "neat" selection to scatter on the surface of concrete. Don't mix an entire batch with it, however, because it's better to have a range of sizes, as mentioned earlier.

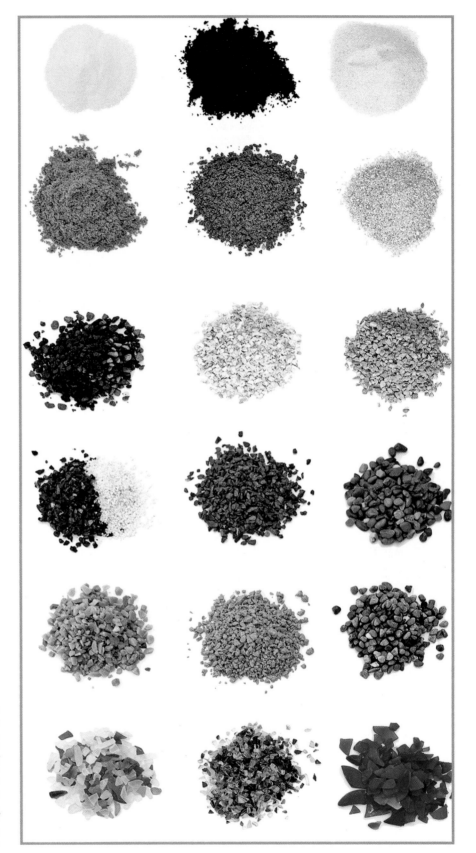

Options for aggregate range from fine powder to big chunks in a rainbow of colors. Top row: white marble dust, black pebble sand, silica sand; second row: tan sand, granite sand, Granusil blasting sand; third row: black pebbles, mother-of-pearl, rose marble; fourth row: black and white marble, green marble, Roan River pebbles; fifth row: Buckskin quartz, cream stone, pea gravel; sixth row: tumbled recycled glass, stained-glass shards, cobalt-blue tumbled glass.

Overview

Adding color to your projects

MOST CONCRETE IS GRAY. But it doesn't have to be. You can add mineral pigments, stains, and even ordinary paint to give concrete the magic of color.

Whatever your approach, be sure to use colorants that stand up to the alkalinity of cement. Besides incorporating pigments and stains sold specifically for concrete, you may be able to use powdered pigments sold in some paint stores. If the pigments are iron oxides, they should work fine: labels may say "ochre," "umber," or "burnt sienna." Wood stains may also work, but for vivid, permanent color your best option is "acid stain," a relatively new product that combines chemically with ingredients near the surface of concrete.

You can also paint concrete, but don't apply oil-based stains or paints until the concrete is thoroughly dry—at least a month old. With water-based finishes, the timing isn't as critical. If you're not sure whether a colorant will work, leave a sample outdoors for a month to see whether it fades noticeably.

For vivid colors beyond earth tones, there's always paint. On this concrete patio, the painted carpet dresses up the space and makes the floor easier to wipe clean.

To create this three-piece bench, the manufacturer tinted a white-cement mixture with yellow pigment and placed it into molds one handful at a time. This created voids, which were filled with a cement-and-water putty tinted a different shade. The effect looks a bit like marble.

Buff (in white cement)

Green (in white cement)

Goldenrod (in white cement)

Mohawk Orange (in white cement)

Buff (in gray cement)

Green (in gray cement)

Goldenrod (in gray cement)

Mohawk Orange (in gray cement)

Preparing concrete with white cement, rather than the standard gray, produces brighter colors. These samples show the effect of 1 pound of pigment per 94-pound sack of cement.

Yellow (in white cement)

Cobalt Blue (in white cement)

Brown (in white cement)

Red (in white cement)

Yellow (in gray cement)

Cobalt Blue (in gray cement)

Brown (in gray cement)

Red (in gray cement)

ADDING INTEGRAL COLOR

Incorporating pigment as you mix concrete is the quickest, most foolproof way to add color. There's no extra labor, and you wind up with a mixture that's tinted all the way through. If any edges on the finished product chip, the newly exposed concrete will blend in.

Buy pigment dispersed in water or as dry powder. Using the liquid form helps ensure even color. However, the widest color selection is available as powder, which is sold in bulk and in bags that disintegrate in a mixer.

In most cases, add pigment with the first batch of mix water. If you are using dry pigment and want to avoid streaks, whisk it with part of the water first. Or add the pigment after the gravel if you are using a motorized mixer (see page 37). If you want streaks of color, stir dry pigment into the other ingredients after they are thoroughly mixed.

How much should you add?

Add pigment until you get a somewhat darker version of the shade you want, because colors lighten as concrete cures. But once pigment totals about 10 percent of the cement, you may find that the color is as deep as it will get. Stop adding pigment at this point. If you're preparing test samples or are pouring your project in stages, measure cement, water, and pigment ratios precisely and keep notes so you can duplicate the color later.

To create the contrasting colors in this driveway-turned-basketball court, the builder framed and poured the red areas, then removed the forms and poured the tan expanses. Because the pigment was added to the other ingredients, it will never wear off.

BROADCASTING DRY PIGMENT

In addition to incorporating dry pigment, you can also trowel it into the surface of concrete as it hardens. By sprinkling on several colors, you can create rich color variations. You may also save money, because you'll use less pigment than you would if you tinted the concrete all the way through.

Use premixed "color hardener" or make your own from pigment, cement, and sand in a 1:6:6 ratio. Reduce

The varied colors in this path were created by broadcasting several different tones of color hardener onto freshly poured concrete. The grout lines look realistic because they were cut out with a grinder and filled with mortar. Doing this reduces the chance that weeds might grow in the joints. The mortar is shallow and has solid concrete underneath.

the amount of pigment if you wish. A homemade mix won't produce color that looks as uniform or trowels on as smooth because the pigment and cement can't be combined as thoroughly.

To broadcast dry pigment, pour the concrete and roughly level it as you would any slab project. Sprinkle on about two-thirds of the pigment mixture. Trowel it in, wait for surface water to disappear, then add the rest of the colorant and trowel the surface again.

To create this patio, the builder began by pouring concrete that was lightly tinted with a buff pigment. He then rolled out a paper stencil to create the look of grout lines and broadcast a slightly different tone of color hardener over it. He used a textured roller to create the rippled surface.

USING ACID STAINS

Acid stains are alchemist tools for coloring concrete. You don't know what they will look like until the job is done.

These stains consist of acidic solutions rich with metallic salts. When you brush, spray, or rub them on concrete, the acid etches the surface, allowing the salts to react with hydrated lime in the hardened concrete. This results in colored compounds permanently bonded to the surface. Each job and even different parts of the same job usually turn out a little different because the final color depends on the aggregate incorporated, the additives used when the concrete was poured, the tools and techniques used to smooth the concrete, and many other factors.

Stains come in shades of black, brown, and blue-green. Some manufacturers warn that persistent moisture might darken some colors, particularly blue-green. Use these stains in indoor areas where the concrete stays dry.

A brown acid stain, in a shade known as Cola, gives this kitchen floor a rich, variegated look reminiscent of burnished leather. Clear wax applied with a buffing machine adds the sheen.

Safety

Read labels and follow all instructions. Acid stains contain hydrochloric acid and other hazardous ingredients, so protect your skin, eyes, and lungs when applying the product. Wear goggles and neoprene gloves. Depending on the situation, you may also need a protective apron and boots as well as a full-face mask fitted with acid/gas cartridges. As with other acids, add the stain to water, not water to the stain, or the solution may spatter or boil. Proper disposal of containers and rinse water is very important.

18

A band of lawn separates a starburst design from the main entry of this house. The sun's rays were created with black and tan acid stains. Nearby paving received a brown stain.

Achieving custom colors

Acid stains are available in only a few stock colors, but it's easy to create custom tones and special color effects.

To soften a shade, dilute the stain with water or acid before applying. To darken or enrich a color, apply a second coat. Multiple coats also even out areas where the first coat didn't penetrate well or where brush strokes show.

To get a design of several distinct colors, cut the outline into the concrete with a 4-inch angle grinder fitted with a diamond blade, or a similar tool. After the staining is complete, you can leave the grooves or fill them with grout.

Acid stains produce blacks, browns, and blue-greens in tones that vary from one manufacturer to the next. This chart shows the selection available from one manufacturer.

VinGreen Lawn Stain
Soft gray-green resembling aged Italian marble

English Red Stain
Terra cotta with rust and soft brown hues

Black Stain
Tortoise shell black with brown marbling

Malay Tan Stain
Buckskin suede tone with caramel marbling

Vintage Umber Stain
Rich earthy brown

Golden Wheat Stain
Amber-hued undertones

Aqua Blue Stain
Soft blue patina with undertones of green

Cola Stain
Reddish-brown, resembling old leather

Shaping concrete

THE FOLLOWING PAGES DISCUSS THE BASICS of molding and shaping concrete, how to prevent cracks, which kind of concrete is best for your needs, and how to trowel and finish the job. Once you understand these basics, you'll be ready to try your hand at the projects described in the following chapter.

Pouring concrete into a mold is the most common shaping method. Design sturdy forms (see example below) that you can remove easily. A light spray of cooking oil will keep molds from sticking to concrete. Use screws or double-head "duplex" nails, placed where you can get to them later.

CASTING ON THE GROUND

You need only an edge form when you cast concrete for a walkway, patio, or decorative edging strip.

Mark the perimeter with string or spray paint. Without disturbing underlying soil, dig straight down at least 2 inches for small projects such as steppingstones. Cast small projects directly on soil. For patios and paths, excavate at least 6 inches to allow a slightly elevated 4-inch slab (minimum thickness) over a 4-inch bed of crushed rock or pea gravel. Adding gravel to the hole before you build the form is easier than shoveling gravel in later.

Preventing problems

Use concrete made with gravel, not a sand mix, for projects cast on the ground. Prevent cracks by breaking long, skinny rectangles and L-shaped sections into squares and blocky rectangles. Divide long sections into smaller ones with special expansion-gap material, or frame sections with rot-resistant wood that you leave in place as a decorative edging.

For more details about pouring concrete next to a house, building large forms, and other complex issues, consult Sunset's *Complete Masonry*.

2 by 4 set on edge

Two layers of benderboard (or use ¼-inch plywood)

Stakes every 3 feet or less; trim flush

Slope of at least ⅛ inch per foot so water runs off

Dirt, gravel, or strips of wood to keep concrete from oozing out

Tip

TO DETERMINE EXPANSION-GAP spacing, multiply the slab's thickness in inches by 2½. The result is the maximum number of feet that should be in a section. For example, a pathway 4 inches thick requires a break every 10 feet.

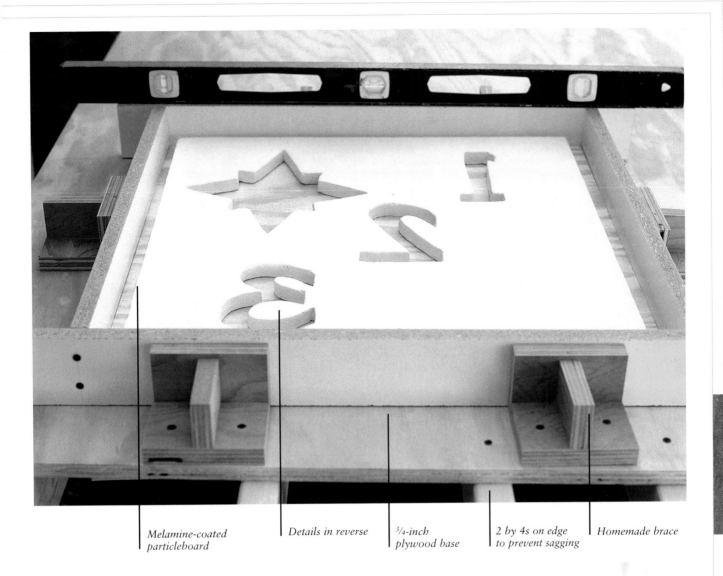

| Melamine-coated particleboard | Details in reverse | 3/4-inch plywood base | 2 by 4s on edge to prevent sagging | Homemade brace |

CASTING OFF THE GROUND

To mold a tabletop, counter, or other slab that's off the ground, you can work either right side up and shape the top surface by hand or right side down and let the mold do the smoothing. If your pour will be face down, you need to build every detail of the mold in reverse.

Either way, begin by building an open box. On face-down projects, ensure a smooth finish by building the form from 3/4-inch-thick particleboard coated with melamine, a plastic that doesn't stick to concrete. Buy 4-by-8-foot sheets or smaller sizes sold as shelving. For more complex shapes, such as sink knockouts, use foam insulation board (with double-stick tape to build up layers, if necessary) or polystyrene foam (Styrofoam). Cut these materials with a knife or saw; shape them with a rasp. Smooth with drywall mud or cover edges with plastic tape or mason's polyethylene tape.

Tip

A LIGHT SPRAY OF COOKING OIL keeps molds from sticking to the concrete. But don't use so much that it puddles.

This fountain was made from rubber molds sold for this purpose. The curb consists of 10 pieces mortared together. Decorative bands of copper around the top of the pedestal add a refined, custom touch.

OTHER MOLDING METHODS

In addition to the materials described on previous pages, you can also build forms from many other materials, including metal, sand, and clay. A trip through thrift-store aisles or a tour of garage sales may yield inexpensive, creative molds for garden pots, birdbaths, and other projects. For example, you could cast concrete in the glass globe of a lighting fixture, then break away the glass when the concrete hardens to reveal a concrete ball or finial. Smooth a rough form, such as a basket, by lining it with plastic. (See page 140 for more ideas.)

Manufacturers also sell ready-made molds for projects such as steppingstones and garden benches (see Resources, page 142).

Creating flexible molds

You can create your own flexible molds with liquid urethane rubber or latex. You can pour, paint, or spray these materials onto a prepared surface, wait for the liquid to stiffen, and then peel off a mirror image. You can then mold concrete to that surface to get a faithful replica of the original—not the reverse. These molds capture fine details and they are reusable.

Liquid urethane rubber stands up to the high alkalinity of concrete much longer than latex. Find the rubber material at hobby and art-supply stores

An artist modeled this sculpture in clay. So that she could create multiple copies, she painted it with several layers of rubber mold material. A white plaster-of-Paris "mother mold" fits to the back of the rubber and adds support when the mold is loaded with wet concrete. The mother mold comes apart, so the casting is easy to remove. "Raven-haired Girl" mold, R.A. Krutch©.

Tip

TO FORTIFY a flimsy mold without creating a "mother mold" from plaster, embed the back in sand or spray it with expanding-foam insulation.

(or see Resources, page 142). Choose a formula that remains quite stretchy if you need to cast a slightly undercut shape. Stiffer formulas last longer, though; they're a better choice if you plan to cast multiples. Be sure to follow safety recommendations.

SCULPTING CONCRETE

The word "pour" is so closely associated with concrete that you might not realize you can skip using a mold and sculpt concrete almost as if it were clay.

Use a sand mix and prepare it quite stiff. Shape with your gloved hands, old spoons and knives, or standard pottery-shaping tools. Just keep in mind that there are several important differences between working with clay and sculpting with concrete.

Hollow sculptures or those with parts likely to break, such as the ears of this rabbit, start as metal skeletons. Add concrete in layers, smoothing and shaping as you go. The first coat must interlock with the metal but doesn't have to be smooth.

Adding strength

Concrete has very little resistance to bending or stretching, and it's prone to cracking on the inside corner of any acute angle. Long or complex shapes require reinforcing, often with a metal armature plus metal mesh (see page 31). A hollow shape is more crack resistant than a solid form, especially if it's large and placed where temperatures fluctuate rapidly, perhaps in a spot where sunshine shifts to shadow.

Layering

Concrete doesn't stand up on its own like clay does; it sags. To create high-relief details, allow one layer to stiffen before you dab on the next. Bagged quick-setting concrete, a specialty sand mix, works especially well if you mix it in batches, one layer at a time. To ensure a strong bond, keep the underlying layers damp and paint the part you are building up with a slurry of 2 parts cement to 1 part water, or with acrylic or latex fortifier (also sold as bonder).

Details begin to emerge with the second coat, which in this case is made of white cement and fine white sand. For smoothing large areas, use a slightly damper mixture than you need when building up details such as a nose or tail.

23

PRESSING CONCRETE INTO A FORM

You can create garden pots and similar items by packing barely damp sand mix against a mold and allowing it to harden there. Because the mix contains so little water, the resulting concrete becomes very strong and should withstand freezing and thawing without cracking. The cast-stone industry uses a similar method for producing exquisitely detailed garden urns, planters, and other items that last outdoors for decades.

This forming method is quite low tech. Besides a sturdy mold that's easy to remove, a mixing container, and a pair of gloves, the only tool you need is a round river rock that fits comfortably in your hand.

The procedure

Preparing the sand mix is a bit tricky. A cement mixer or even a shovel or hoe won't moisten the dry ingredients evenly. Factories use mortar mixers, which have paddles. For small projects, work in the water with gloved hands. Stop when the mixture is just moist enough to hold its shape when squeezed. The consistency resembles pie crust before you gather it into a ball.

Press some of the mixture into the bottom of the mold and pound it with the rock into a layer 1 to $1\frac{1}{2}$ inches thick. You'll feel the sand mix compacting. Work your way up the sides, adding material as you go and keeping the thickness as uniform as you can. Do not produce a layer

A barely moist sand mix, packed into forms, produced the crisp details on this 55-inch-wide urn and its stand, a reproduction of a piece designed by Frank Lloyd Wright. Concrete formed in this way gets its color largely from the sand that's used, not from pigment. White cement with tan sand resembles sandstone.

over 2 inches thick; it won't compress adequately.

When the shape is complete, cover it with plastic wrap. Remove the mold as early as the next day, but keep the sand mix damp for at least several days.

Variation

Prepare a slightly wetter mix with water alone or (for more frost resistance) half water and half acrylic or latex fortifier. The mixture should still be very stiff. A little at a time, pack it into a mold with a stick.

Tip

TO REINFORCE A LARGE POT or other object made with this method, add polypropylene or other fibers to the sand-cement mixture.

CARVING CONCRETE

In addition to molding concrete, you can also shape it by carving. The effect looks very much like carved stone, but the effort it takes is far less. If you carve your design when the concrete is stiff but not yet very hard, you won't generate dust and you won't need special stone-carving tools. A kitchen knife, a spoon, an old saw blade, or a nail will work fine. As the piece becomes harder and harder, you can add progressively finer details and create an even smoother surface.

For a rather rough look, create a carving blank from quick-setting cement or a standard sand mix. If you want fine details or a smoother surface, sieve the dry ingredients through a window screen to remove large particles. For an ultrasmooth, glistening surface, use a homemade sand mix with marble dust as the aggregate.

Timing

If you plan to use the carving technique to add details, remember that concrete is easiest to carve soon after it sets. But since it won't have developed much strength at that point, treat the piece gently. If you are using a mold, design it so you can pull away the sides and begin carving without moving the piece from its base. On a 70-degree day, it may take 3 hours for a standard sand mix to stiffen enough to carve. Quick-setting cement may be ready in half an hour.

Techniques

To give your piece a uniform texture, scrape off the crusty surface cement with a serrated knife or a reciprocating-saw blade. Or leave some areas untouched to create contrasting textures. Carve the main shape with a knife. Refine details with other tools, as needed. When you're done, lightly brush the surface with a whisk broom or a toothbrush, depending on the piece's size. Cover with plastic and keep damp.

As the concrete hardens, you can add finer details and smooth the surface with a rasp, sanding sponge, or wet-dry sandpaper. To keep down dust, work on a damp surface.

Concrete that's stiff but not yet hard is ready to carve. A kitchen knife slices through a design outlined with a homemade tool.

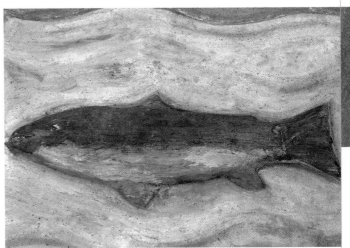

To color the carving, the artist mixed equal amounts of white cement and pigment and sprinkled them onto the still-damp concrete. After dribbling water onto the pigment, she smoothed it with a butter knife.

You can use common tools to carve concrete while it's still relatively soft.

Preventing cracks with reinforcement

SOME CONCRETE PROJECTS need metal or fiber reinforcing to keep them from cracking. Other projects do fine without it. Understanding why concrete cracks and how reinforcement works will help you decide when to add it. When in doubt, put it in. Reinforcing is cheap insurance.

Adding too much water to the initial mix resulted in these surface cracks.

Preventing surface cracks

Concrete often develops small surface cracks that are caused by excess water in the mix. Adding thin fibers to the mix reduces or eliminates this problem, as does limiting the water you add or substituting acrylic or latex fortifier for some of the water.

Creating stiffness

Concrete doesn't crush easily, but it has little ability to withstand bending or stretching. Instead of flexing, it cracks. If you are pouring concrete onto undisturbed ground, you don't need to add reinforcing. But you should use iron reinforcing bars ("rebar"), welded-wire mesh, or expanded-metal lath to stiffen a project such as a countertop with an overhang, a garden bench seat that spans several feet, or a precast countertop that you may knock while moving. Fibers also add stiffness, but not as much as metal.

When its support eroded, this concrete cracked from lack of stiffness.

Reinforcing weak shapes

As it cures, concrete slowly shrinks to account for the water it loses. Adequate expansion gaps (see page 20) give it a way to do this without cracking. The gaps also allow the concrete to expand when temperatures rise. But long, skinny rectangles and interior corners on L-shaped projects still often crack because the ends don't shrink in tandem. Avoid problems by redesigning your project into squares and short rectangles, if possible. (Round shapes are even stronger.) If you can't avoid weak shapes, reinforce them to help the concrete move as one piece. Use rebar or welded-wire mesh with gravel-based concrete and welded-wire mesh or expanded-metal lath with sand mixes.

To round a corner, this concrete walkway was cast into an L shape. It cracked at the corner.

USING FIBER REINFORCING

When you open a bag of fiber reinforcing for the first time, it's hard to believe that something so tiny can do so much. Whisper thin and generally about a half-inch long, fibers made of nylon, polypropylene, or special fiberglass help stiffen concrete and protect it from fine surface cracks.

Polypropylene fibers are the most readily available. Concrete-supply companies sell them in 1-pound bags that disintegrate in a cement mixer. Manufacturers recommend using one or two bags per cubic yard of concrete, so for a single bag of concrete mix you'll need just a few pinches. Using more won't create problems, however.

Add fibers after you have incorporated some of the mix water. If fibers poke out from the surface once your project is complete, wait for the concrete to cure, then burn off with a small propane torch.

Glass fibers

If you add glass fibers to your mix, be certain they are alkali resistant so they won't break down. Don't improvise by using chopped strands of fiberglass insulation.

Bagged mixes

Besides adding fibers to bagged mixes or concrete you mix from scratch, you can also buy products with fibers. These include "fiber cement mix," which contains gravel and can be used for projects at least 2 inches thick, and "surface-bonding cement," designed for thin applications.

The polypropylene fibers sold for strengthening concrete don't look like much until you realize that each bundle contains countless superfine strands.

This massive urn, 5 feet wide, has no structural reinforcement other than polypropylene fibers. It's a reproduction of urns that anchor corners of Frank Lloyd Wright's Frederick C. Robie house.

USING METAL REINFORCING

Adding a few pieces of metal reinforcing may make all the difference in keeping your project intact. But it won't prevent cracks caused by lack of adequate expansion gaps (see page 20).

Although rebar plays a big role in fortifying structural features built from concrete, it's far less common in decorative projects of the type featured in this book. One reason is that adding rebar to relatively thin slabs can actually cause the concrete to crack. Rebar close to a surface will rust if the concrete absorbs moisture, and rust takes up more space than bare metal. So rusted rebar will push on the concrete and break it if the concrete is not thick enough, especially if it's made without gravel. In thin pours, rebar can also do what's called "ghost," or cause white lines to show on the surface over the metal.

Still, rebar does have uses in decorative projects. Where concrete needs additional stiffness, it's often the best solution. Just be sure to match the reinforcing to the thickness of your project so at least 1 inch of concrete surrounds the metal. Allow a bit extra to be safe.

If your goal is to knit together the concrete so it expands and contracts as one unit, wire mesh may work better than metal bars.

REBAR AND THREADED ROD

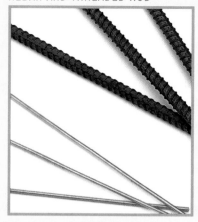

WELDED-WIRE MESH

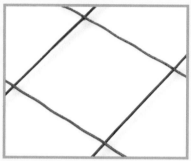

EXPANDED-METAL LATH

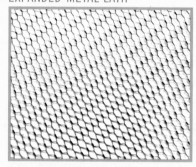

HARDWARE CLOTH

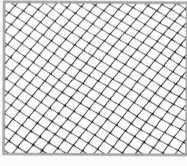

CHICKEN WIRE

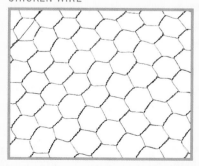

Types

For projects similar to those in this book, your metal-reinforcing choices range from quite stiff to rather flexible:

REBAR: Use ½-inch rebar for projects more than 3 inches thick, ⅜-inch rebar for projects about 2½ inches thick.

THREADED ROD: Also known as "pencil rod," these ¼-inch rods substitute for the rebar on projects thinner than 2½ inches. Sold where fasteners are displayed.

WIRE: Substitute for rebar on even thinner projects. Nick with a file or bend in kinks to help concrete grip it.

WELDED-WIRE MESH: Also known as "WWR" or "remesh." Sold flat, in 4-by-7-foot sheets. Get 4-inch or 6-inch openings.

EXPANDED-METAL LATH: Also called "diamond mesh." Sold in 27-by-96-inch sheets. The gauge rated at 2.5 pounds per square yard works well with sand mixes. Buy it galvanized.

HARDWARE CLOTH: Sold in rolls with openings as small as ¼ inch. Buy it galvanized.

CHICKEN WIRE: For sculptures and free-form projects. Can be bent into complex shapes more easily than hardware cloth. Sold in rolls of various widths, usually with 1-inch openings.

WORKING WITH REBAR

Use rebar primarily to add stiffness to concrete that is subjected to forces that might cause it to stretch or bend. For example, a garden bench that's supported by posts at both ends might need to stretch a bit if it has to carry too much weight in the middle. And an overhanging countertop, supported only on one end, might flex if someone stood on it to change a light bulb.

Tools

Professionals use special tools for shaping rebar and twisting wire, but for small, occasional projects you can improvise.

❖ Cut rebar with a hacksaw. To save effort, stop partway through and snap pieces apart.

❖ If you need multiple bends, for example, to skirt a sink shape, cut short pieces and make one bend per piece. Then wire the pieces together.

❖ To join pieces, overlap the ends by at least several inches and twist 22-gauge tie wire tightly around them. Use lineman's pliers.

Cut rebar with a hacksaw, jigsaw, or reciprocating saw. You can stop partway through and snap the waste part free.

Hold intersecting lengths of rebar together with wire, twisted tight with lineman's pliers. If three-dimensional armatures, such as skeletons for sculptural projects, still wobble, wrap the joints again, in a criss-cross fashion.

A rebar "chair" holds metal reinforcing at the proper depth. You can also support rebar on small plugs of concrete.

Placement

For the types of projects in this book, you can generally embed the rebar halfway down in the concrete. But for maximum strength, follow these strategies, provided there will still be at least 1 inch of concrete beyond the metal:

❖ To stiffen a section between two posts, place rebar one-third of the way down.

❖ For slabs supported only at one end, aim for two-thirds of the way down.

❖ To strengthen a weak shape, put rebar in the middle. Place it in the direction that needs stiffening.

For cast-in-place projects, professionals use premade "chairs" to hold rebar at the proper level. You can bend similar supports from stiff wire or hang the rebar from wire fastened to wooden strips tacked across the top of the form.

For molded projects such as countertops, you can also tap the rebar into the concrete after you pour it. For this method, level and vibrate the concrete to remove air bubbles (see page 37). Then quickly set the rebar on top and tap it in, using a marked stick as a gauge.

Cut expanded-metal lath with aviator's snips. To keep it from cutting you, pull up on the left piece with your free hand. You may also need to hold down the right piece with a clamp or your foot.

WORKING WITH METAL MESH AND LATH

Metal mesh helps tie concrete together so slabs move as one unit. But to accomplish this, the openings in the metal must be big enough for the largest aggregate to slip through easily. Mesh is especially useful in decorative projects created with sand mixes, which lack the built-in strength that standard concrete gets from gravel.

Tools and techniques

Use metal-cutting snips, such as aviator's snips, to cut most weights of metal mesh. Wear leather gloves. You can also cut expanded-metal lath with a circular saw fitted with a diamond blade. Support the mesh on boards spaced slightly apart and cut between them. Wear goggles and long sleeves to shield yourself from flying bits of hot metal.

Placement

Cut metal mesh so that it stops 1 inch shy of all edges. Bridge L-shaped sections with a single piece of mesh cut to fit, or place a separate piece on each leg and overlap the pieces at the corner. For three-dimensional projects such as sinks, bend the mesh around corners. It's fine to use a different piece of mesh for each corner. Mesh should be placed in the middle of the concrete. For slabs, pour half the concrete and roughly level it. Place the mesh on top and add the rest of the concrete. Don't allow the first layer to set up before you add the second.

Projects such as this concrete hassock are easiest to build with polystyrene foam as the core. Buy blocks at packing-supply companies or build up thick pieces from foam insulation board layered with double-stick tape. Cut the foam with a bread knife, drywall saw, or other long-blade tool, and refine the shape with a wire brush or a rasp. Wrap the form with metal mesh. Weave in 20-gauge wire to hold the mesh in place. This project, like others that need extra strength, will get a second layer of mesh after the initial coat of concrete has set. See page 23 for details on how to apply the concrete.

REINFORCING COMPLEX SHAPES

To create sculptures, birdbaths, and other complex shapes, you may need both a stiff skeleton and enough mesh to fill out the shape.

A skeleton, or an armature, for concrete works differently than bones do in an animal. The support concept is the same, but with concrete the torso is boxed in rather than held up with a backbone. If the armature will be less than 2 feet tall, you can build it from heavy wire. For really large pieces, use pipes screwed together with plumbing fittings. For projects sized in between, use rebar if your piece includes thin shapes and polystyrene foam if it's blocky.

Building a rebar skeleton

Sketch your project as a stick figure to help you plan. Then cut the pieces so ends overlap about 1 inch and fasten them with tightly twisted 22-gauge tie wire. Rest outstretched features, such as arms or tails, on top of the basic frame pieces so the stiff metal and not the twisted wire provides support. Combine materials if it's useful. Create a curved detail with a wire skeleton, for example, but use rebar for the main support.

Tip

SPRAY YOUR COMPLETED REBAR skeleton with primer paint designed to keep rusty surfaces from corroding further. Because rust expands more than the metal it replaces, the paint will protect your project from cracking.

Build armatures, such as this support for a birdbath, slightly undersize. The shape will "grow" as you add metal mesh to fill spaces between the rebar and then coat the mesh with concrete.

Working with concrete

WITH YOUR MATERIALS
GATHERED AND YOUR FORM
OR ARMATURE IN PLACE, at last
you can think about adding
the concrete. Your first deci-
sion: whether to buy a mix or
use a scratch recipe. Choose a
method that allows the entire
batch to be mixed at once, if
possible.

❖ Truck delivery: Standard
  mixers usually won't deliver
  less than 1 cubic yard—
  enough concrete to pour
  a 4-inch-thick pad 8 feet
  by 10 feet. A "short pour"
  truck, if available can
  deliver smaller amounts.

❖ Portable mixer: One with
  a 3.5-cubic-foot capacity
  will handle several bags
  of concrete.

❖ Hand mixing: Use a wheelbarrow or mortar mixer
  or even a dishpan for
  extremely small batches.
  Wear gloves.

*Mix concrete in a mortar tray or wheelbarrow by pulling the
dry mixture into the water little by little. Work the dampened
material back toward the dry area, almost as you would
when kneading bread. With your shovel or hoe, repeatedly slice
through the mixture to break up any lumps.*

CALCULATING QUANTITIES

Use math or muscle to figure out how much
concrete you need. For the math method,
calculate the volume by multiplying your project's length times width times height. If you
measure in inches, divide the result by 1,728
to convert to cubic feet (the dimension used
on bagged mixes) or by 46,656 to change to
cubic yards (for truck delivery). For complex
molds, mentally divide the project into simple
shapes and calculate their volumes individually.
Or use the muscle method: measure how much
sand fits inside the mold. A 5-gallon bucket
is a useful measure; it holds two-thirds of a
cubic foot.

MIXING CONCRETE FROM SCRATCH

As with food, there are literally hundreds of different formulas for concrete. But for projects like those in this book, two basic recipes work well. As you gain experience, you can adjust them to create specialty mixes.

The two basic recipes differ primarily in the size of aggregate they contain. Basic Concrete Mix contains gravel, so it's suitable for projects such as countertops or pathways that are at least 2 inches thick.

Use Basic Sand Mix for thinner slabs and for projects that call for sculpting or carving.

BASIC CONCRETE MIX

- ❖ ½ part cement
- ❖ 1 part pea gravel (³⁄₈ inch or less)
- ❖ 1 part sand
- ❖ Approximately ¼ part water

Yield: about 1½ parts concrete

BASIC SAND MIX

- ❖ 1 part cement
- ❖ 2 parts sand
- ❖ Approximately ½ part water

Yield: about 2 parts sand mix

Variations

You can tweak the basic recipes in several ways:

- ❖ Add ½ part more cement plus a little additional water to create a creamier cement. *Benefit:* produces a smoother finish with less effort.

- ❖ Replace up to half the water with acrylic or latex fortifier. *Benefit:* creates denser concrete that's less porous and less likely to crack. For sand mix: also allows applications ½ to 1 inch thick.

- ❖ Add polypropylene fibers. *Benefit:* protects against surface cracks. For sand mix: also adds stiffness.

- ❖ Replace part of the cement (up to 15 percent) with fly ash or metakaolin and reduce the amount of water. *Benefit:* makes concrete denser, easier to shape, and less prone to surface cracks.

Creating freeze-resistant concrete

Ice crystals occupy about 9 percent more space than the water that's in them. So when concrete absorbs water and then freezes, the ice can literally split the concrete. Several steps eliminate or at least reduce this concern:

- ❖ Add an "air-entraining" product. Available from concrete-supply companies, this material forms tiny bubbles that act as safety valves, giving ice crystals room to expand. Requires truck delivery or motorized mixing.

- ❖ Replace some of the mix water with acrylic or latex fortifier.

- ❖ Barely dampen the concrete and pound it in place (see page 24).

- ❖ Use a bagged mix that contains waterproofing ingredients.

- ❖ Coat the cured concrete with a sealer.

USING BAGGED MIXES

Concrete made from bagged mixes costs more per cubic foot than concrete you mix from scratch. But using the bagged products frees you from searching for specialty ingredients and from buying them in greater quantities than you need.

Manufacturers rarely reveal what's in their mixes, but you can look on the label or tech sheet for the strength (shown as psi, or pounds per square inch). Although this number specifically refers only to crush resistance, you can use it as an overall indicator of durability and abrasion resistance.

The projects in this book note specific branded products, but others may also work. However, it may be difficult to determine whether similar-sounding products from different companies are identical. Call manufacturers' help lines (see Resources, page 142) if you're not sure.

CONCRETE MIX

❖ Gray Portland cement, sand, and gravel

❖ Good for paths, steppingstones, and other projects at least 2 inches thick

❖ For countertops or other high-impact, smooth projects, add ½ gallon cement powder per sack of mix

CONCRETE COUNTER MIX

❖ White Portland cement, sand, marble dust, metakaolin, and other ingredients

❖ Designed for countertops, but has many other uses

❖ Can be mixed quite dry and pressed into shape

❖ White color tints well

❖ Polish for a terrazzo look

SAND MIX

❖ Gray Portland cement and sand, in a ratio of approximately 1 to 3

❖ Good for countertops and other poured projects less than 2 inches thick

❖ Can also be used as a ½-inch or thicker coating for old concrete

❖ Can be carved, stamped, or sculpted

NON-SHRINK PRECISION GROUT

❖ Gray Portland cement, sand, expansive materials, and other additives

❖ Develops high strength even when mixed quite soupy so it flows into intricate molds

❖ Great for precast countertops

❖ Must be mixed mechanically

❖ Stiffens in 15 to 25 minutes, depending on temperature

FAST-SETTING CONCRETE MIX

❖ Gray Portland cement, sand, and additives

❖ Sculpt as it begins to harden

❖ Or pour into a form, unmold when set, and carve details

❖ Stiffens in just 5 to 10 minutes; mix small batches

HIGH EARLY STRENGTH CONCRETE MIX

❖ Gray Portland cement, sand, gravel, and additives

❖ Good for countertops, hearths, and other poured projects at least 2 inches thick

❖ Contains a higher than usual percentage of cement, so it's easier to finish

GLASS BLOCK MORTAR MIX

❖ Fine silica sand, mason's lime, white cement, and waterproofing ingredients

❖ Use as a topping on projects not subject to abrasion; too soft for casting

❖ White color works well with pigments

CONCRETE RESURFACER

❖ Gray Portland cement, sand, polymers, and other ingredients

❖ Gives a fresh cement-based coat to old concrete

❖ Mix thin and spread by squeegee or brush, or add less water and trowel on up to $\frac{1}{2}$ inch deep

❖ Can be tinted and textured; suitable for layering different colors

Overview

35

MIXING CONCRETE

The trickiest aspect of mixing concrete is adding the right amount of water. One minute, the mixture seems too stiff. So you add a bit more water. Then, suddenly, it's too soupy. Test the consistency with a simple slump test. Cut the bottom off a foam or paper cup and set the cup upside down. Fill it with concrete, tamping as you go. Lift the cup straight up. If the pile slumps to about three-fourths of the cup's height, the mix is right for pouring into a form. If it slumps more, add more dry mix. If it slumps less, add water. For sculpting or packing against a mold, the concrete should stay about the same height as the cup.

ONE LAST CHECK

Before you mix concrete, step back and make sure everything is ready.

FORMS OR MOLDS

- ❖ Sturdy enough?
- ❖ Level or at proper angle for water to run off?
- ❖ Faucet and sink knockouts or other special features in place?
- ❖ Rebar fully supported or mesh cut to shape?
- ❖ Forms coated with oil or other form-release material?
- ❖ Surrounding areas protected with plastic?
- ❖ Tools at hand for vibrating air bubbles out of the mix?

MIXING AND POURING

- ❖ Materials on hand?
  - – Cement
  - – Aggregate
  - – Measured amount of mix water

  - – Additives (fortifiers, fibers, pigment, etc.)
  - – Decorative material, such as inlays
- ❖ Tools and containers ready and in useable condition?
  - – Cement mixer, wheelbarrow, or dishpan
  - – Shovel or hoe
  - – Hose and buckets
  - – Smoothing tools (flat board for initial leveling, wood and/or metal floats, edger)
- ❖ Safety gear available?
  - – Disposable respirator
  - – Rubber gloves
  - – Goggles

FOLLOW-UP

- ❖ Plastic cover to keep project damp?
- ❖ Person assigned to rinse tools and containers promptly?
- ❖ Storage system planned for rinse water, especially if there are additives that should not go into soil?

PLACING AND LEVELING CONCRETE

Because chemical bonds begin forming as soon as water contacts cement, ensure a strong result by minimizing your handling of the damp concrete. Shovel or dump it as close as possible to where the finished product will end up.

For most projects, fill the mold partway, taking care to pack concrete into edges and around detail areas, such as faucet knockouts. Stop and remove air pockets (see below). Then fill the mold the rest of the way and repeat the air-removal process. You should wind up with a mold slightly overfull.

Removing air pockets

On projects that require smooth edges, you must work air pockets out of the concrete as soon as it's poured. Professionals use special gear, but these methods also work:

❖ Tap the bottom and sides of the mold with a hammer.

❖ Hold a palm sander against the mold, working your way around it.

❖ If you have tools that run on compressed air, substitute an air hammer for the sander.

❖ Place the mold on a series of dowels before you fill it. Then (with a helper) rock the filled mold back and forth, sending air bubbles toward the sides. Knock the sides with a hammer.

Watch the concrete carefully as you do these things. When you see the concrete slump and tiny air bubbles rise to the surface, stop. Overvibrating will cause big aggregate to sink to the bottom and water to rise.

If you are reinforcing your project with expanded-metal lath or other mesh, fill the form halfway, then just slip the mesh into place and resume filling. Keep the mesh 1 inch from all edges.

Screeding

To remove excess concrete from the mold, "screed" the surface by moving a stiff, straight board back and forth across the top of the form. On wide projects, have one person at each end of the board if possible.

Toss excess concrete onto low spots and screed the surface a second time if needed. Do not try to make the surface smooth at this point, though. Let the concrete sit awhile.

Use a straight 2 by 4 to level the concrete. Sawing back and forth helps compact the mix and even out rough spots. Fill any gaps with the excess that collects along the front of the 2 by 4.

Tip

WITH A 3.5-CUBIC-FOOT MIXER, it's best to put in about three-fourths of the water first. Add gravel, then pigment, then sand, and finally cement, mixing after each addition. After you add the cement, squirt one burst of water into the mixer to reduce dust and prevent clumps. Tilt the tub back and forth periodically as the machine mixes. Add the final water in small amounts until the consistency is like oatmeal.

SMOOTHING AND FINISHING

The key to achieving a smooth, durable finish on concrete is not rushing to begin troweling. Wait until surface water disappears and the concrete loses its sheen. Depending on the mix and the weather, that may take 30 minutes to several hours.

FLOATING: Use a wooden or magnesium float, placed flat. Trowel the surface to push any protruding aggregate below the top skim of cement paste. The concrete should become smooth but still look slightly textured. Stop at this point if you want a nonskid surface or plan to finish the concrete with a broom or other texture tool.

FIRST TROWELING: Wait for any water raised by the float to disappear. Then smooth the surface with a trowel. Hold the leading edge up and press down harder than you did the first time. Stop at this step for a pleasantly smooth surface on projects such as a garden bench.

SECOND TROWELING: Wait again for any surface water to disappear. Then trowel a second time. Hold the leading edge even higher and press down even more. The surface should become almost glossy, ideal for countertops.

Edging

To create a finished edge on a poured-in-place slab, run a trowel or putty knife between the form and the concrete to separate them. Then work an edger (a tool with a curved edge) along the form to round the outside edge of the concrete. Use short strokes so you can work surface grit down below the surface. Finish by smoothing the edge with a long, light pass.

Sealing and waxing

Depending on how you will use your project, you may want to apply a sealer and wax to minimize stains. Read labels to make sure you choose a sealer appropriate for concrete. Beeswax and other waxes add a nice final flourish to indoor projects.

Floating

Second troweling

Clear wax protects and adds luster to this floor, which was colored with acid stain.

FIXING PROBLEMS

Leave your project in the mold for at least several days to help ensure even curing. Keep the concrete damp during this time and for several days after you remove the mold.

If you discover air gaps, fill them with a putty made of cement and water plus any pigment. Because the water content of the putty will differ from that in the original mix, patches tend to dry darker than the surrounding concrete. If you used gray cement in the original, you can prevent this by using white cement in the patch. You can also patch holes with a contrasting color.

Polishing

Hand sanding with water lubrication works surprisingly well if you tackle the job 3 to 10 days after the pour. If sanding causes aggregate to lift out, wait a day before resuming. Use wet-dry sandpaper or diamond pads, which cut faster and last longer. Start with 120 grit and move to 220, then go to 440. See the following chapter for some tips on how to create a terrazzo-type finish.

Small circular holes, known as "bug holes," often appear on molded surfaces, especially those made with a sand mix instead of gravel-based concrete. Wait several days for the concrete to harden before filling these holes. If they are large, use a putty mixture, as explained in the text above. To fill small holes, dampen the surface, sprinkle with cement (plus any pigment), and rub in with a piece of burlap. Using fresh burlap, rub off the excess.

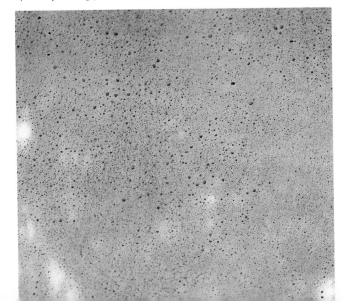

Instead of trying to make patched areas blend in, you can opt for a contrasting color and make it part of the design. The marbled look of this table results from placing tinted concrete into a mold one handful at a time and then patching voids with a contrasting color.

Patterns and styles

Mention "decorative concrete" to some people and they'll assume you're talking about large expanses of paving stamped and colored to look like stone or brick. That is indeed one of the possibilities. But concrete also adapts to a wide variety of other surface treatments, including many that do not require expensive, specialized equipment. In this chapter, you will see examples of finishes that you can use on a wide variety of projects. The smooth finishes are suitable for countertops, tabletops, and sinks. Save the heavily textured or surface-pigmented finishes for wall tiles, fireplace surrounds, garden art such as fountain backsplashes, and similar uses where the surface won't wear down or become clogged with dirt. One caveat: to keep people from slipping, avoid overly smooth surfaces on floors or paving that may become wet.

Terrazzo

THIS SAMPLE:
White cement, white marble dust, black and green marble chips, mother-of-pearl; Davis Colors #3685 green added to two sections in different concentrations; brass strips

To create classic terrazzo, embed marble chips or mother-of-pearl in a cement mix and grind the surface smooth. Large projects are best done by pros with multihead polishing machines. But you can tackle small projects yourself if you're willing to accept slight indentations and have access to a hand-held grinder or stone polisher equipped for wet sanding with diamond pads. If you do it yourself, lay out the design so you can divide large areas with metal gauge strips, which also set the depth and control cracks. Combine marble dust, marble chips, and cement in equal proportions. Mix with water and concrete bonding adhesive into a stiff goo. Smooth over dampened concrete. Keep damp 3 days, then polish wet. Start with 50-grit pads and go to 400 or higher.

Glass terrazzo

THIS SAMPLE:
Buddy Rhodes Concrete Countertop Mix plus Davis Colors #6058 reddish-brown, confetti glass shards

Press glass shards into freshly poured concrete to create another type of terrazzo. Place a paper pattern on the surface to confine the glass to the design area. Embed the pieces with a trowel and force some of the surface cream over them. Trowel smooth. Wait 3 days, then polish. This sample was created with stained-glass waste and Buddy Rhodes Concrete Countertop Mix, which incorporates marble chips. A 50-grit hand diamond pad exposed the marble in this mix, creating a subdued terrazzo effect. Exposing the pattern took more work. We used a stone polisher.

YOU NEED:

- ❖ Basic Sand Mix or Basic Concrete Mix, page 33, or a bagged mix (with ½ gallon added cement per bag if you use standard bagged concrete mix)
- ❖ Broken tiles
- ❖ Sponge, preferably hydrophobic polyester, the type sold at mason's-supply stores or for smoothing wallpaper; it rinses out easily

Set bits of tile or pottery into damp concrete or sand mix to create mosaic designs. You can also create mosaics with mastic and grout, as you would set tile, but the direct method allows you to embed a design in a small section of a path or other concrete project. Spread and level the concrete or sand mix. Dampen and place the pieces, then jiggle each one to embed it fully. Smooth around edges with a barely damp sponge. Blot surrounding areas if you want to create a slightly textured surface. As the concrete stiffens, wipe tiles clean. Rinse and squeeze out the sponge frequently. Wipe surfaces gently; sand grains can scratch glazed tile.

THIS SAMPLE:
Basic Sand Mix made with half white and half gray cement, glazed tiles

YOU NEED:

- ❖ Basic Sand Mix or Basic Concrete Mix, page 33, or a bagged mix (with about ½ gallon extra cement if you use standard concrete mix)
- ❖ Glass or other flat mosaic pieces
- ❖ Adhesive shelf paper

Place glass or other decorative bits into a mold to cast a mosaic design into a countertop or similar project that you make upside down. Use only absolutely flat pieces for this technique, and press them to adhesive shelf paper or attach with washable glue. Either step will keep the pieces from shifting and prevent cement from seeping underneath. As with any molded project, the design will appear in reverse, so adhere the surface you want to expose. When the design is in place, prepare a sand mix. Make hamburger-size patties and add them one by one. Pat each one down and jiggle the mold to make sure the mixture fills in around the edges of the mosaic.

THIS SAMPLE:
Basic Concrete Mix made with ¼-inch gravel and Davis Colors #860 black pigment; dichroic and cobalt-blue glass from Messolini Glass Studio

White cement dust

YOU NEED:

❖ Basic Sand Mix or Basic Concrete Mix, page 33, or a bagged mix (with ½ gallon extra cement if you use standard bagged concrete mix)
❖ Dry or liquid pigment, if desired
❖ White cement
❖ Hammer

THIS SAMPLE:
PakMix Concrete Mix with additional gray cement and Davis Colors #860 black pigment, white cement

Toss a handful of white cement into the bottom of a mold to produce cloudlike puffs on a countertop or similar surface. Make the contrast vivid, as in this black-and-white sample, or go for a more subdued look by mixing the concrete with half white and half gray cement and no pigment. To preserve the pure white puffs, place sand or concrete mix into the mold by hand in hamburger-patty–size chunks. When you've covered the entire bottom with about a ½-inch layer, hit the mold with a hammer to release air bubbles. Then fill the mold the rest of the way and tamp around edges with a hammer.

Broom finish

YOU NEED:

❖ Basic Concrete Mix or Basic Sand Mix, page 33, or a bagged mix (with ½ gallon extra cement per bag if you use standard concrete mix)
❖ Dry or liquid pigment, if desired
❖ Broom of suitable texture
❖ Float or steel trowel
❖ Edging tool

Run a broom over fresh concrete to create straight or curved grooves that add interest and improve slip resistance. For a rough surface suitable for steps and ramps, smooth the concrete with a wooden or magnesium float, wait for the concrete to become fairly solid, and then go over it with a stiff broom. For a smoother texture that's friendlier to bare feet, smooth the surface with a steel trowel before you sweep with a fine-bristle broom. With either method, frequently rinse the bristles and shake out excess water. To create the smooth, rounded edge shown on this sample, go around the perimeter with an edging tool immediately after you float the concrete. Do it again after you sweep.

THIS SAMPLE:
Quikrete Concrete Mix prepared with added gray Portland cement and Quikrete Buff Cement Color

YOU NEED:

❖ Basic Concrete Mix or Basic Sand Mix, page 33, or a bagged mix (with ½ gallon extra cement per bag if you use standard concrete mix)

❖ Dry or liquid pigment, plus additional dry pigment

❖ Burlap

Fold a tinted cement mix into dry pigment one handful at a time to create a mottled look somewhat reminiscent of marble. Use sand mix or concrete mix. Place the pigmented handfuls into a mold, then level and trowel the surface as usual. (The molded face is shown here.) If the dry pigment contains lumps, the molded face may be left with voids. Wait several days before you fill them with a mixture of cement, pigment, and water. Buff away excess filler with a piece of burlap.

THIS SAMPLE:
Basic Sand Mix made with white cement and Davis Colors #5447 yellow, streaked with Davis Colors #160 red

YOU NEED:

❖ Smooth, dry concrete at least 14 days old

❖ Acid stain

❖ Safety gear (goggles and neoprene gloves; depending on job conditions, you may also need protective clothing, boots, and a full-face mask fitted with acid/gas cartridges; add a dust mask if you will make saw cuts)

❖ Baking soda

❖ Sawdust or an acid-resistant vacuum to collect residue and rinse water

❖ Diamond blade in a circular saw (if you want saw kerfs)

❖ Acid-resistant or disposable paintbrush

❖ Plastic bucket for the stain, with a plastic tray to collect drips

Paint acid stains onto concrete to produce mottled, translucent color. These stains, which contain hydrochloric acid, are generally applied by professionals. Read the manufacturer's entire technical sheet before you attempt to use them. Have the necessary safety gear and a way to collect residue and rinse water. To create the tile look shown here, score the surface with a diamond blade in a circular saw. (Wear a disposable respirator for the dust.) Apply stain. Novices should use a brush, not a sprayer. Wait for color to develop, neutralize the residue with baking soda, and clean the surface as directed by the stain manufacturer. Fill cuts with grout, if you wish.

THIS SAMPLE:
Old pigmented concrete stained with Scofield Weathered Bronze and Padre Brown acid stain in alternating squares

Swirls of color

YOU NEED:

- ❖ Basic Concrete Mix or Basic Sand Mix, page 33, or a bagged mix (with ½ gallon extra cement per bag if you use standard concrete mix)
- ❖ Dry or liquid pigment
- ❖ Premixed color hardener or a mixture of dry pigment, cement, and fine sand whisked together in a 1:6:6 ratio
- ❖ Broom of suitable texture
- ❖ Edging tool
- ❖ Disposable respirator
- ❖ Trowel

Add contrasting color to dress up other finishes, such as this broom finish. Create the base color by adding dry or liquid pigment to a sand or concrete mix. Pour and level the concrete. After surface water disappears, sprinkle a contrasting color onto the surface. Use premixed color hardener (also known as "dry shake"). Or, for small projects where you want only a few contrasting swirls, whisk dry pigment with cement and fine sand. Wearing a disposable respirator for the dust, toss a small amount of the pigment mixture onto the concrete. Wait for the pigment to moisten. Trowel it in. Finish with a broom and an edger tool, as described on page 46.

THIS SAMPLE:
Base: Quikrete Sand Mix with Davis Colors #160 red pigment, applied as a topping over old concrete; homemade color hardener with Davis Colors #5447 yellow

Contrasting textures

THIS SAMPLE:
Basic Sand Mix prepared with Davis Colors #160 red pigment

YOU NEED:

- ❖ Basic Sand Mix or Basic Concrete Mix, page 33, or a bagged sand or concrete mix (with ½ gallon extra cement per bag if you use standard concrete mix)
- ❖ Steel trowel
- ❖ Stipple-texture paint roller with handle
- ❖ Plastic wrap and tape

Create contrasting textures to enliven pavement, fireplace surrounds, and other projects. For the rippled surface on the bottom, go over the concrete with a textured roller after the surface water disappears but before the surface is completely stiff. Professionals use embossed-steel cylinders, but for small jobs use a roller with a stipple texture. Wind plastic wrap over the roller and tape the ends. To create the smooth surface on the top, polish the concrete with a steel trowel, as described on page 38.

YOU NEED:

❖ New or existing concrete base
❖ Basic Sand Mix, page 33, or a bagged sand mix
❖ Dry or liquid pigment, if desired
❖ Large paintbrush
❖ Trowel

Add rough texture that resembles hand-split sedimentary rock, such as bluestone, by splattering new or old concrete with sand mix. Clean old concrete thoroughly. Coat new or old concrete with bonding adhesive and wait for it to become tacky. Meanwhile, prepare Basic Sand Mix or a bagged sand mix with dry or liquid pig-

ment, as desired. With a large brush, splatter the mixture onto the surface so that clumps are about $\frac{1}{2}$ inch deep. Trowel very lightly, allowing some depressions to remain. This finish works well on garden paths where winters are not severe. It may not stand up to heavy vehicle traffic or frequent freezing.

THIS SAMPLE:
Base: Basic Sand Mix with Davis Colors #5447 yellow; topping is the same but uses white cement

YOU NEED:

❖ Basic Sand Mix or Basic Concrete Mix, page 33, or a bagged mix (with $\frac{1}{2}$ gallon extra cement per bag if you use standard concrete mix)
❖ Dry or liquid pigment, if desired
❖ Trowel
❖ Brick jointer or other imprint tool

Push designs into concrete that's partially set but still pliable. Options include far more than handprints (although those are fun, too). You can create a design similar to this one with a $\frac{3}{8}$-inch brick jointer, a tool normally used to smooth mortar. Begin by preparing a sand or concrete mix as usual. Add dry or liquid pigment, if you

wish. Pour and level the mix. Wait for the surface water to disappear, then trowel smooth. Create the design by pulling the tool across the surface, as if drawing.

THIS SAMPLE:
Basic Sand Mix made with white cement and Davis Colors #5447 yellow

Stamped design

YOU NEED:

- ❖ Basic Sand Mix, page 33, or a bagged sand mix
- ❖ Liquid or dry pigment, if desired
- ❖ Concrete bonding adhesive, if you are pouring thin pieces
- ❖ Trowel
- ❖ Non-absorbent items to use as stamps

THIS SAMPLE:
Basic Sand Mix made with white cement, #70-grit white silica sand, and Quikrete Concrete Bonding Adhesive, plus pigment: Davis Colors #677 brown, #5376 green, #5447 yellow, and #160 red

Create interesting designs by stamping concrete while it is still quite pliable. Use non-absorbent objects with simple shapes. For these tiles, we used the bottoms of plastic drinking cups. Prepare Basic Sand Mix or a bagged sand mix, with dry or liquid pigment if desired. Replace some of the mix water with con-crete bonding adhesive if you are pouring thin pieces such as these tiles, which vary from ½ to ¾ inch thick. Pour and trowel the mixture smooth, wait for it to stiffen slightly, then stamp. If water puddles in the first place you stamp, wait a little before you proceed.

Embossed effect

THIS SAMPLE:
Basic Sand Mix prepared with half white and half gray cement; slip made with white or gray cement mixed with Davis Colors #8058 reddish-brown, #677 brown, and #5084 gold

YOU NEED:

- ❖ Basic Sand Mix or Basic Concrete Mix, page 33, or a bagged mix (with ½ gallon extra cement per bag if you use standard concrete mix)
- ❖ Poster board
- ❖ Craft knife or scroll saw (to cut cardboard)
- ❖ Cooking-oil spray
- ❖ Liquid or dry pigment
- ❖ Trowel
- ❖ Extra cement

With a cardboard template and cement "slip," you can mimic handmade clay tiles. Cut your design out of poster board, removing areas that will be raised. Spray the cardboard with cooking oil. Blot. Prepare a sand or concrete mix, tinted as you wish. Pour and level. When the mixture has stiffened slightly, place the template onto the surface. Trowel smooth, forcing the surface cream of cement and fine sand to fill in around the cardboard. A half-day or so later, when the concrete is stiff but not yet dry, remove the cardboard and color the recessed areas with cement slip—cement, pigment, and water the consistency of cream. For glossy color, drib-ble the slip, don't brush it.

Textured mat

YOU NEED:

- Basic Sand Mix or Basic Concrete Mix, page 33, or a bagged mix (with ½ gallon extra cement per sack if you use standard concrete mix)
- Dry liquid pigment, if desired
- Burlap
- Trowel
- Spray bottle with water

To create a skid-resistant and beautiful surface, emboss the surface with a texture. Professionals use plastic mats to imprint textures that mimic a wide variety of stones, but improvised solutions also work. Burlap, shown here, creates a refined, uniform grid. Pour and level a concrete or sand mix. Wait for surface water to disappear, then trowel. When the surface becomes quite firm, mist a sheet of burlap with water and shake out the excess liquid. Smooth the fabric over the surface. Tamp with a trowel, then remove the burlap. Use this texture on wall surfaces and fireplace surrounds. It may be too fine to stand up to heavy traffic.

THIS SAMPLE:
Bagged concrete mix with added white cement and Davis Colors #3685 green

Pigmented shape

YOU NEED:

- Basic Concrete Mix or Basic Sand Mix, page 33, or a bagged mix (with ½ gallon extra cement if you use standard concrete mix)
- Additional dry cement for spot color
- Dry or liquid pigment as integral color, if desired, plus additional dry pigment for spot color
- Stamp or mold materials
- Spray bottle with water

Dust interesting materials with pigment and use them as either stamps or molds to imprint concrete with both texture and vivid color. Because the pigment stays within depressed parts of the design, it should be fairly durable even though it is only at the surface. Select items that are relatively stiff and not too porous. This sample was made with leaves of globe thistle (*Echinops ritro*). The leaves were misted with water, sprinkled with dry pigment, and placed on the bottom of a mold. With leaves or similar materials, add concrete in handfuls so the design doesn't move and the pigments don't blur. Remove from the mold and peel off the mold materials after a day or two.

THIS SAMPLE:
Basic Concrete Mix with Davis Colors #5376 green; leaves dusted with Davis Colors #160 red, #5447 yellow, and #5376 green

Exposed aggregate

THIS SAMPLE:
Basic Concrete Mix made with Roan River ³/₈-inch pea gravel and Quikrete Buff Cement Color

Brush away surface cement to reveal the gravel and sand that normally hide within concrete. Use standard bagged concrete mix or incorporate decorative rocks in your own mix. Pour and level the concrete. Wait about 6 hours, until it has set. Then scrub off the surface with a stiff scrub brush. Rinse with a fine hose spray or wash out the scrub brush as needed and brush again. Avoid brushing too deeply; stones embedded less than halfway will fall out. An exposed aggregate finish is well suited to driveways and garden paths since it resists wear, slips, and glare. Because stones don't stain as easily as cement, exposed aggregate finishes are also relatively stain resistant.

Seeded aggregate

THIS SAMPLE:
Bagged sand mix tinted with Davis Colors #160 red and seeded with Roan River pea gravel

Scattering decorative stones onto newly poured concrete or sand mix is another way to create an exposed aggregate finish. You use the decorative pieces more efficiently, and you have the option of broadcasting the stones over only part of the surface as long as your pour is narrow enough for you to reach the area you want. To create a design, cut a pattern from brown paper. Mist with cooking-oil spray and place onto the surface. Scatter pebbles into the open areas. If any land on the paper, brush them to where you want them. With a trowel, embed the stones, as shown in step 5 on page 102. Wait 6 hours, then proceed.

YOU NEED:

- ❖ Basic Sand Mix, page 33
- ❖ Concrete bonding adhesive or a slurry of cement and water
- ❖ Paintbrush
- ❖ Decorative pebbles
- ❖ Plywood scrap
- ❖ Hammer
- ❖ Margin trowel or other small trowel

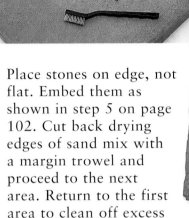

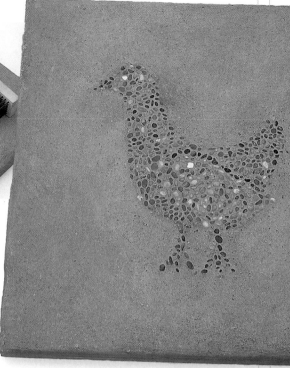

Place pebbles individually to create designs. Use sand mix for steppingstones. For paths or patios, pour concrete and top that with sand mix. Working on 1 or 2 square feet at a time, paint the concrete with bonding adhesive or a cement-water slurry. Cover with sand mix ½ inch deeper than the pebbles are tall.

Place stones on edge, not flat. Embed them as shown in step 5 on page 102. Cut back drying edges of sand mix with a margin trowel and proceed to the next area. Return to the first area to clean off excess cement, as shown in step 6 on page 102.

THIS SAMPLE:
Basic Sand Mix made with half white and half gray cement, ³/₈-inch coral pebbles

YOU NEED:

- ❖ Basic Sand Mix, page 33, or bagged sand mix
- ❖ Dry sand
- ❖ Sieve or flour sifter
- ❖ Decorative pebbles
- ❖ Spray bottle with water

Reverse pebble mosaic

THIS SAMPLE:
Basic Sand Mix with Davis Colors #160 red, Roan River coral, and Mexican black stones

Cast a pebble mosaic in reverse in a mold to give yourself maximum working time. With this method, you add sand mix only after all stones are in place, so you can take your time and create elaborate designs, including those that cover the entire surface. Spread sand over the bottom of the form. Using a sifter helps ensure an even layer. Make the sand about as deep as you want the pebbles to be exposed; it must hold them on edge as you place them. When stones are set, mist with water. With gloved hands, carefully place hamburger-patty–size clumps of sand mix over the design. Press down without tipping the stones. Finish filling the form. A day or two later, invert and remove the form. Brush away any excess sand.

Inlays

Add metal, semi-precious stones, or other inserts for a custom touch on countertops, hearths, and similar surfaces that are cast upside down in a mold. If you use coins or other textured inlays, smear a little plasticine clay over the faces to keep concrete out of the voids. Use the clay to stick the inlays upside down to the mold bottom. Attach flat inlays with washable glue. For the pattern here, stuff short copper pipes with cement mix. Pat to draw up the cement cream. Invert and place in rows. Fill around pieces with patty-size handfuls of cement mix, vibrate to remove air bubbles, then fill the mold the rest of the way and vibrate again. Sand smooth with a wet grinder or stone polisher (see Resources, page 142).

Carved decoration

Cut incised designs into barely set sand mix to create textured designs suitable for wall surfaces, fireplace surrounds, garden art, or even paving. Draw the design on paper first, if you wish. Then prepare, pour, and level the sand mix. Trowel smooth after surface water disappears. Once the mixture stiffens, in about 6 hours, place the paper on the concrete and trace over the drawing to transfer the lines to the concrete. Or carve freehand with a kitchen knife, brick jointer, pottery tool, or other implement. Add contrasting color to the incised areas, if you wish. This design sparkles from a sprinkling of bronze powder, sold at art-supply stores.

Carved and filled design

YOU NEED:

- ❖ Basic Sand Mix, page 33, or bagged sand mix
- ❖ Dry or liquid pigment
- ❖ Concrete bonding adhesive (over old concrete or if final step is delayed)
- ❖ Paper pattern
- ❖ Cooking-oil spray
- ❖ Carving tools or margin trowel
- ❖ Trowel

Fill a carved design with a contrasting color of sand mix to create a pattern that won't wear off. For the base color, spread sand mix at least $\frac{1}{2}$ inch thick over existing concrete or pour a slab that's at least $1\frac{1}{2}$ inches thick. Cut a paper template with holes where the contrasting color will be. Oil the pattern and set it in place when the mix is stiff. Slice straight down $\frac{1}{4}$ inch or more but not all the way through. Carve out with a putty knife, spoon, or margin trowel. Fill with fresh sand mix in a different color. (Coat with bonding adhesive first if the carved layer is more than 24 hours old.) Trowel smooth. Lift the pattern.

THIS SAMPLE:
PakMix Sand Mix with Davis Colors #160 red in the base

Recipes

Incised design

YOU NEED:

- ❖ Bagged concrete resurfacing material
- ❖ Dry or liquid pigment, if desired
- ❖ Squeegee of a size suitable for your project
- ❖ Paddle mixer, drill, and 5-gallon bucket for mixing
- ❖ Cut-off nail pounded into a wooden handle
- ❖ Styrofoam pad
- ❖ Soft cloth

Scratch a design into a thin cement topping to give old concrete the look of stone. Incorporate existing cracks into your design because they will inevitably transfer through. Begin by cleaning and dampening the old concrete. Prepare bagged resurfacing material using a paddle mixer in a drill (or a whisk for small batches). With a squeegee, spread the topping about $\frac{1}{4}$ inch deep. Wait a few hours for it to stiffen. Kneeling on a Styrofoam pad, scratch the design with a cut-off nail. Buff the surface with a soft cloth, working debris from the scratches back into the lines. It will harden there and look like grout.

THIS SAMPLE:
Quikrete Concrete Resurfacer with Davis Colors #677 brown

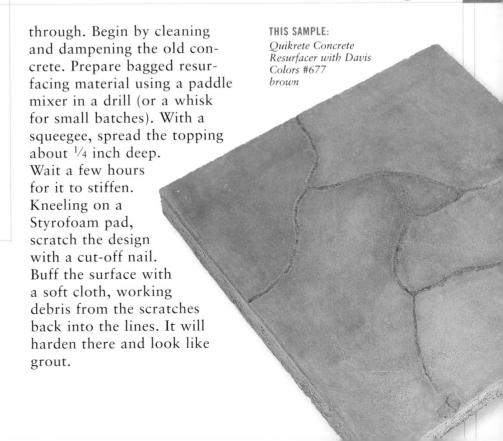

Stenciled white cement

THIS SAMPLE:
Basic Concrete Mix made with Davis Colors #860 black

YOU NEED:

❖ Basic Sand Mix or Basic Concrete Mix, page 33, or a bagged mix
❖ White cement
❖ Dry or liquid pigments if desired
❖ Paper stencil
❖ Cooking-oil spray
❖ Trowel
❖ Sieve or flour sifter
❖ Plastic wrap

Create a snow scene or another design by covering fresh concrete or sand mix with a paper stencil and then sifting white cement over it. Cut the design from brown paper and spray with cooking oil. Prepare a sand or concrete mix and pour and trowel it as usual. When there is no surface water, position the paper. Sift white cement over the surface. Remove the stencil after a day, but leave the piece covered with plastic for several days. Areas you don't cover will wind up white, with a crunchy texture. This finish is durable enough to be scrubbed, but it won't stand up to heavy traffic. Use it on a fireplace surround, wall tiles, or as part of garden art.

Stenciled mortar lines

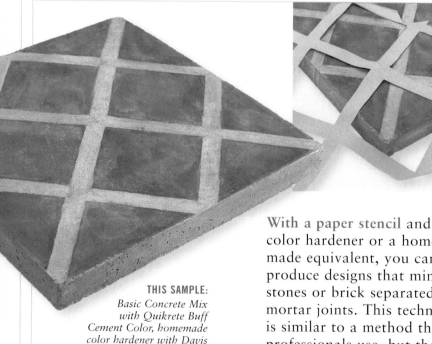

THIS SAMPLE:
Basic Concrete Mix with Quikrete Buff Cement Color, homemade color hardener with Davis Colors #160 red

YOU NEED:

❖ Basic Sand Mix or Basic Concrete Mix, page 33, or a bagged mix (with ½ gallon extra cement if you use standard concrete mix)
❖ Brown paper
❖ Cooking-oil spray
❖ Color hardener or pigment, sand, and fine sand whisked together in a 1:6:6 ratio
❖ Trowel

With a paper stencil and color hardener or a homemade equivalent, you can produce designs that mimic stones or brick separated by mortar joints. This technique is similar to a method that professionals use, but their stencils are a yard wide and 325 feet long. For a small project, cut a stencil from brown paper and spray it with cooking oil. Prepare concrete or sand mix, then spread and smooth it as usual. When there is no surface water, spread the stencil over the surface. Press edges so they don't lift. Wearing a respirator, toss the pigment mixture over the surface. Trowel it in without lifting the stencil. Remove the paper after the concrete stiffens.

YOU NEED:

- ❖ Basic Sand Mix or Basic Concrete Mix, page 33, or a bagged mix (with ½ gallon extra cement if you use standard concrete mix)
- ❖ Brown paper
- ❖ Cooking-oil spray
- ❖ Color hardener or pigment, sand, and fine sand whisked together in a 1:6:6 ratio
- ❖ Trowel

Adapt the paper stencil technique to make designs that go beyond trying to mimic stones or brick. Cut brown paper freehand or in a precise pattern and use it as described on the bottom of page 54. Simple designs work best. Intricate stencils tend to lift as you trowel the dry color into the surface. Different troweling techniques change the way the color appears. If you want fairly uniform color, trowel back and forth and in a circular motion. Besides spreading the color, this also works pigment deeper into the surface. If you want streaks, trowel only back and forth.

THIS SAMPLE:
Basic Sand Mix applied as a topping over old concrete, homemade color hardener with Davis Colors #5447 yellow

Recipes

YOU NEED:

- ❖ Basic Sand Mix or Basic Concrete Mix, page 33, or a bagged mix (with ½ gallon extra cement if you use standard concrete mix)
- ❖ Leaves or other stencils
- ❖ Cooking-oil spray
- ❖ Color hardener or dry pigment, sand, and fine sand whisked together in a 1:6:6 ratio
- ❖ Trowel

Improvise stencils by using leaves or other found items that are relatively nonporous but still flexible. You must be able to smooth the stencil over the surface without having the edges lift as you trowel color into the surrounding concrete or sand mix. One bonus of this method: by pressing down with a trowel on the stencil, you can also transfer the stencil's surface texture to the concrete. Follow the basic procedure for working with paper stencils, described on page 54.

THIS SAMPLE:
Basic Sand Mix made with Davis Colors #160 red, applied as a topping over old concrete; homemade color hardener with Davis Colors #677 brown

Plastic bag mold

Line a mold with wrinkled plastic sheeting to cast a network of small depressions into concrete. Fill them with contrasting color and you'll have a slab that resembles natural stone streaked with minerals. Cut open a plastic garbage bag or use similar lightweight plastic. Arrange it in the mold, smoothing or clumping folds and wrinkles as you wish. Prepare a sand or concrete mix. Add it to the mold one handful at a time. Remove the mold after several days and

THIS SAMPLE:
Basic Concrete Mix made with Davis Colors #860 black; filler contains Davis Colors #160 red

fill depressions with a mixture of cement, pigment, and water. Use a wide putty knife. (If you have large depressions, add fine sand to the filler.) Buff away excess with burlap.

YOU NEED:

- ❖ Basic Sand Mix or Basic Concrete Mix, page 33, or a bagged mix (with ½ gallon extra cement if you use standard concrete mix)
- ❖ Plastic garbage bag or plastic sheeting
- ❖ Dry or liquid pigment
- ❖ Extra cement
- ❖ Wide putty knife
- ❖ Burlap

Molded objects

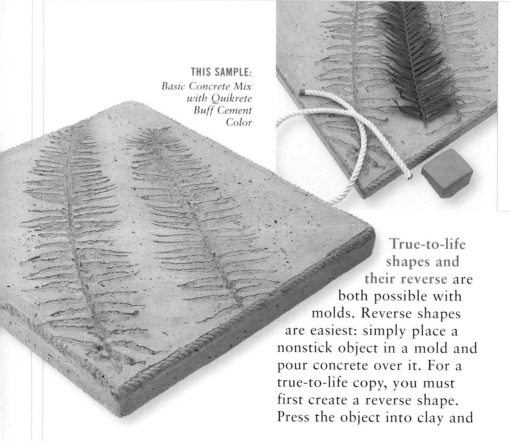

THIS SAMPLE:
Basic Concrete Mix with Quikrete Buff Cement Color

True-to-life shapes and their reverse are both possible with molds. Reverse shapes are easiest: simply place a nonstick object in a mold and pour concrete over it. For a true-to-life copy, you must first create a reverse shape. Press the object into clay and

then use the clay as the mold. This sample shows both techniques. Fern fronds placed at the bottom of a mold left holes in their shape. Rope, pressed into plasticine clay around the edges of the form, left indentations that the concrete filled. The rope appears true to life, but it's made of concrete.

YOU NEED:

- ❖ Basic Sand Mix or Basic Concrete Mix, page 33, or a bagged mix (with ½ gallon extra cement if you use standard concrete mix)
- ❖ Fern fronds, rope, or other shapes you want to mold
- ❖ Cooking-oil spray, if concrete would stick to mold materials
- ❖ Plasticine clay, available at art-supply stores

YOU NEED:

- ❖ Basic Sand Mix, page 33, or a bagged sand mix
- ❖ Pottery clay
- ❖ Cooking-oil spray
- ❖ Rolling pin
- ❖ Bamboo or other imprint materials or modeling tools

Use clay on the bottom of a mold to cast intricate shapes. Oil-rich plasticine clay works well because it doesn't dry out or stick to concrete, but it's relatively expensive. We used ordinary pottery clay, which is water based. Cover it tightly with plastic when not in use or it will shrink and crack. Roll out the clay and press objects into it, then remove them and spray the shaped clay with cooking oil. Place hamburger-size patties of sand mix over the clay and pat into a layer about ½ inch deep. Hammer the mold from underneath and around edges, or roll it back and forth on dowels to work out bubbles. Finish filling the mold. Wait at least a day to unmold.

THIS SAMPLE:
Basic Sand Mix made with half white and half gray cement; design created by pressing bamboo stalks and leaves into clay; diluted black latex paint was sponged on to accentuate the design

Recipes

Cardboard shapes

YOU NEED:

- ❖ Basic Sand Mix or Basic Concrete Mix, page 33, or a bagged mix (with ½ gallon extra cement if you use standard concrete mix)
- ❖ Dry or liquid pigment, as desired
- ❖ Cardboard
- ❖ Blue painter's tape (optional)
- ❖ Craft knife or scroll saw
- ❖ Glue stick or other washable glue
- ❖ Cooking-oil spray
- ❖ Plastic wrap

Create slightly raised designs on molded surfaces by placing cardboard cutouts on the bottom of the mold. Cut the cardboard with a craft knife. Or, for multiple copies, pile sheets of cardboard on top of each other and tape the edges with blue painter's tape; then cut with a scroll saw. Spread washable glue over one side of the cardboard and stick it to the bottom of the mold. Spray both the cardboard and the surrounding mold with cooking oil. Wipe up any puddles. Mix and add concrete or sand mix and finish it as usual. Cover with plastic for a day. Unmold and peel off the cardboard.

THIS SAMPLE:
Basic Sand Mix made with white cement and Davis Colors #5237 gold

Projects for your home and garden

Indoors and out, concrete can find a home at your house. Because of its incredible versatility, you may choose it for a simple project, such as a steppingstone, or for a far more elaborate project, such as a sink or fireplace surround. This chapter includes design ideas as well as step-by-step instructions for a range of projects. If you're new to working with concrete, you may want to start with projects such as the steppingstone path or any of the garden pots. Then move up to more challenging projects. Those shown here incorporate a variety of techniques, allowing you to adapt the directions to build other projects of your own design. You can also vary the surface treatments to incorporate features shown in the previous chapter.

Countertops

AMONG ALL THE WAYS to use decorative concrete indoors, countertops are probably the most popular. That is because concrete has the solid look of natural stone but, because you pour it yourself or order it custom-made, you can incorporate special features, such as an integral drainboard next to a sink. For the most scratch resistance, add metal trivets near a stove and use a finish in which most of the surface cement is sanded off, exposing aggregate underneath.

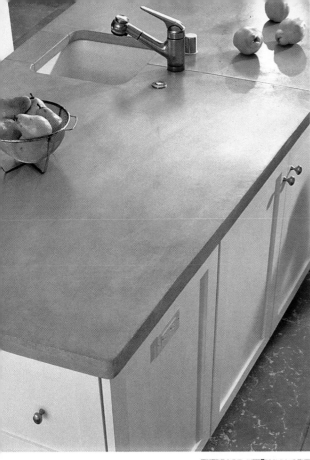

ABOVE: *Several shades of gold combine on this island countertop, giving it an especially rich look. Besides providing a generous work area, the countertop doubles as a breakfast spot.*

TOP RIGHT: *A copper edge band frames this island countertop. To create the marble effect, the builder mixed light-blue concrete and placed it in the form one handful at a time. After removing the mold, he filled voids with a darker paste of cement and water.*

RIGHT: *Curves are easy to create in concrete, and the shape makes a countertop such as this one especially useful as a place for guests to gather as dinner is being prepared. As with round dining tables, a curved counter always has room for one more person.*

OPPOSITE, BELOW: *It's easy to add special features to concrete countertops. The owners of this kitchen collected and positioned maple leaves, then had them cast into place by the professional who built the countertop.*

TOP LEFT: *Six kinds of seashells and a starfish are found among the pebbles that adorn this bathroom countertop, which was built for a house near the Pacific Ocean. The contractor added black pigment to the concrete, scattered the shells, and coated the surface with an epoxy sealer.*

MIDDLE LEFT: *Black concrete and white concrete were mixed separately, then poured together to create the dramatic look of this outdoor countertop. The white portions were later stained to take on a reddish color.*

BOTTOM LEFT: *Too big to be cast in one piece, this island countertop consists of five sections with a diamond-shaped piece at the center. The installers filled the seams with grout so that the countertop would echo the look of the tile floor.*

TOP RIGHT: *Built for a vacation cottage by the beach, this thick concrete sink and countertop give an Asian flair to a small, spare bathroom.*

ABOVE: *Although it looks massive, the base of this kitchen island is made from relatively thin pieces of concrete that box in a support post that runs up the middle. A metal bracket, just visible underneath the overhang, supports the cantilever. Concrete countertops $1^{1}/_{2}$ inches thick, like these, can extend out only about 10 inches without added support or cracks may develop. The countertop and base are both tinted a custom ash color and hand troweled.*

LEFT: *The custom edge on the countertop helps this kitchen island appear more like furniture than standard cabinetry.*

This project features a cast-in-place countertop with an optional terrazzo finish flecked with bits of white marble, mother-of-pearl, and cobalt-blue glass. Casting the countertop in place lets you skip both the heavy lifting and the "upside down and backward" thinking involved in precasting into a mirror-image mold. But troweling the surface smooth does require skill. Practice on other projects first.

A cast-in-place countertop

The countertop rests on a base of $\frac{1}{2}$-inch-thick cement board, enabling you to keep the concrete 1 inch thick except at the edges, which are just enough deeper to hide the cement board. The result is a normal-height countertop that's easily supported by standard cabinets. Reinforcing consists of galvanized-steel stucco lath, so you must use aggregate small enough to fit through the openings. We used Buddy Rhodes Concrete Counter Mix, which contains white cement and bits of white marble, but a standard sand mix would be fine. We troweled blue recycled glass and a few handfuls of mother-of-pearl into the surface and sanded it a few days later by hand, because a polishing machine would have made a mess in the room.

DIRECTIONS

1 Make a template by outlining the shape of your countertop on cardboard. The edges should be flush with the sides of the cabinet. If the counter is bigger than a sheet of cement board, mark joints on the template; they must be placed over cabinet walls. Also mark the sink outline using the template packaged with it.

2 Using the sink template as a guide, cut a plug from foam insulation at least 1½ inches thick to keep the sink free of concrete. A jigsaw or bandsaw works well. Sand edges of the foam and wrap them with plastic tape (see Step 5, page 70).

3 Cut the cement board to fit. For straight cuts, score a line with a utility knife or a knife made from cement board. Snap the sides into a fold and cut through the remaining mesh, as shown.

4 Cut curves with a jigsaw fitted with a wood blade. The blade will wear out fast; have a spare.

5 Along the top of the cabinet sides, screw on some scraps of wood flush with the cabinet top. Drape plastic over the cabinets and place the cement board on top. Then screw down through the board into the wood scraps using drywall screws. Attaching the board this way makes the counter easy to remove if you or a later owner wants to redecorate. Attach the foam plug in a similar way.

6 To guard against cracks appearing in the countertop, cover seams with the mesh tape sold for use with cement board. The tape has an adhesive backing, so it stays in place.

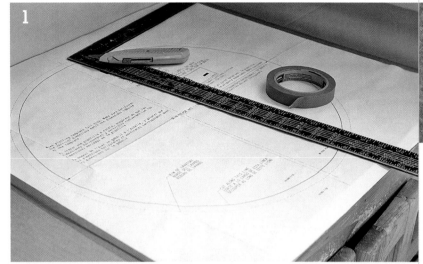

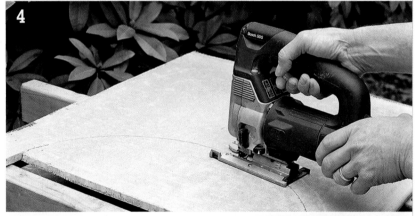

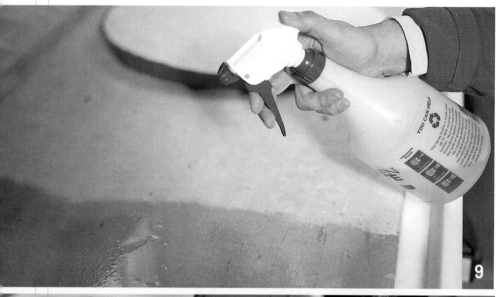

7 With aviator's snips, cut 2½-pound galvanized-steel stucco lath to match the countertop, minus a 1-inch gap along all edges, including all around the sink. If you need multiple pieces, overlap the lath by a few inches.

8 Tack a board 1 inch thick along the back edge to create a guide when you screed the concrete. Plan to cover this later with a backsplash.

9 Before you mix the concrete, dampen the cement board with water. If the cement board dries out, repeat this step just before you fill the form. But blot up any puddles.

10 Prepare Basic Sand Mix, page 33, or a bagged sand mix. With a putty knife, take a little of the prepared mix and press it down into seams covered with mesh. By hand, pack more of the mixture into the edge form. Work quickly to fill the rest of the form halfway.

11 Place the wire mesh. With a float, lightly press it into the bottom layer, just enough so the wire doesn't curl. Make sure it isn't too close to the edges. Then fill the form the rest of the way.

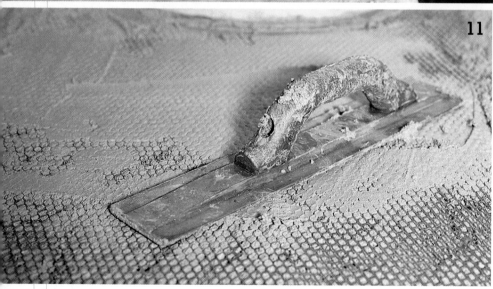

12 With a hammer or stick, tap along the edge band to release air bubbles. Then level the concrete with a straight board as you would for any poured project.

13 Immediately sprinkle glass pieces, mother-of-pearl, or other inlays on the surface. (If you are not going for a terrazzo finish, see page 38 for tips on troweling a surface smooth.)

14 Embed the inlays by troweling over them. To eliminate gaps around their edges, trowel until they are completely covered with the cream of cement and fine sand that is on the surface.

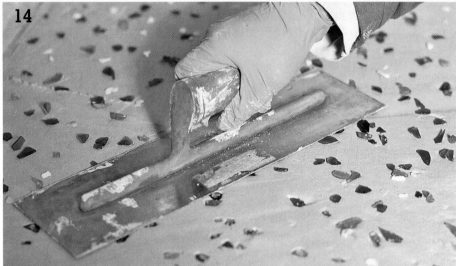

15 Cover the countertop with plastic. For the next three days, periodically mist the concrete to keep it damp.

16 Remove the edge form and cut out the sink plug. Then begin polishing with wet-dry sandpaper, diamond pads, or some solid aluminum-carbide blocks. Start with 100- or 120-grit abrasive and work up to 220 and then 440. If sanding ejects whole pieces of sand or other aggregate, delay this step for another day. Keep handy a pan of water and a sponge (preferably the type sold for masonry jobs) so you can keep the surface damp and periodically wipe away the slurry you will create. Stop sanding when you like the effect.

17 If you see gaps that you don't like, fill them with a paste of cement and water. Allow them to harden for a few days. Polish with wet-dry sandpaper.

18 Seal and wax the counter before you use it.

This countertop was cast upside down in a mold, a process that virtually guarantees a top that's perfectly smooth. Designed for a small home office, the counter's curved shape helps eliminate a feeling of being boxed in. The molded edge, created with a piece of plastic garden edging, adds to the lightweight look. We used a terrazzo-type finish on this project, but many of the other surface treatments shown in Chapter 2 are also possible.

A countertop cast upside down

Build the form from melamine-coated particleboard, which is smooth and won't stick to concrete. The plastic edging is also a nonstick material, so you don't need to coat the mold with cooking oil or other form-release material. Be sure to brace the edging, as shown on page 21, so the plastic doesn't bow out from the pressure of the wet concrete.

DIRECTIONS

1 When you build a countertop upside down in a mold, all details need to be made in reverse. For a simple project like this, make a cardboard template and mark which side goes up. Draw in any details, such as cutouts for electrical cords or places where the counter's shape needs to change to skirt window trim. Then flip over the cardboard, transfer your marks, and build the form to match that side. Cut the outline of the countertop out of a sheet of melamine-coated particleboard.

2 Cut 2½-pound galvanized-steel stucco lath to match the bottom of the mold, but leave a 1-inch gap at all edges, including around any cutouts.

3 Trim plastic garden edging to match the thickness of your countertop (1½ inches works well) plus the thickness of your form material. Using that same width, cut strips of melamine-coated particleboard to make the straight sides of the mold. With drywall screws, screw the bottom of the edging to the perimeter of the countertop mold. Use a block marked at the right height to help you keep the top edge an even 1½ inches above the base.

4 On the inside of the mold, fill gaps between the edging and the mold with plasticine clay. If you want a rounded-over top edge on the countertop, press spaghetti-type strands of the clay along the bottom of the edge and trim them into a concave shape with a potter's tool.

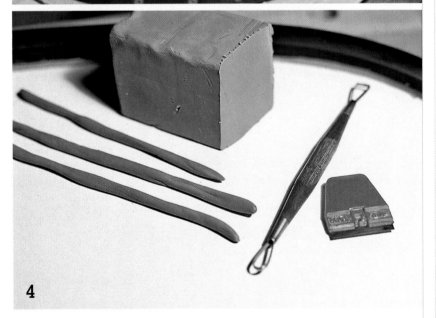

5 From rigid foam insulation, cut plugs for cord holes or other spaces you want to keep free of concrete. Wrap the edges with plastic tape and screw the foam into place on the bottom of the mold, using long drywall screws. Tape over all screwheads so concrete does not plug the hole.

6 If you want a terrazzo effect on your countertop, sprinkle decorative aggregate into the mold. We used mother-of-pearl along edges and dark green marble in the center. The amount of mother-of-pearl shown here turned out to be a bit too much along the front edge, which had gaps that we later had to fill.

7 Place concrete into the form one handful at a time so that the decorative pieces remain evenly distributed and don't get pushed into a pile. Work quickly, particularly if it's a hot day. Fill the mold halfway, then add the mesh and finish filling the mold, as shown in Step 11 on page 66.

8 Pound up on the counter from underneath or rock the form back and forth to work out air bubbles. Tap along the sides as well. Then level the top with a board. When surface water disappears, trowel the surface smooth.

9 Cover the countertop with plastic for three days. Remove the edge forms. With a helper or two, tip the counter upright. The bottom of the mold should slip free. Brush off the workbench and smooth carpet pad over it. Then lower the counter right side up. Cut out the foam plugs.

10 For a terrazzo finish, sand off the surface cement to expose the decorative aggregate. Work on a damp surface to eliminate dust. Start with 100- or 120-grit hand diamond pads, wet-dry sandpaper, or aluminum-carbide blocks. You could also use a stone polisher hooked to a hose. If polishing ejects whole pieces of sand, delay this step for a day or two.

11 Once you have exposed the aggregate, inspect the countertop. If there are holes, mix cement (and pigment, if you used it) with water to a puttylike consistency. Smooth on the mixture with a putty knife. For small holes, mist the surface and sprinkle with dry cement. Rub it in with burlap. Use fresh pieces to wipe off the excess.

12 If you are creating a terrazzo finish, proceed with finer grits (probably 220 and then 440) after the patches have hardened for a day or two. Clean the concrete thoroughly and allow to dry. Seal and wax the countertop before you use it.

This cast-in-place countertop is similar to the one shown on page 64, but it has an undermounted sink, a custom-made bullnose edge, and a troweled finish.

Like the countertop shown earlier, this project calls for an inch of sand mix reinforced with expanded-metal lath on top of a base of $\frac{1}{2}$-inch cement board. With such a thin pour, cracks are likely to develop if the countertop is longer than about 6 feet. Ours is nearly 11 feet, so we added a thin piece of stainless steel to make two sections.

Countertop with undermounted sink

Undermounted sinks typically are fastened to the bottom of countertops with clips, which in turn are held in place by short screws in plastic expansion caps fitted into holes in the countertop material. Because the caps would extend only into the cement board, we opted to rest this sink on a rim cut from plywood. We installed the sink first, then poured the countertop over it.

To form the bullnose edge, which drops down to cover the edge of the cement board, we used $1\frac{1}{2}$-inch plastic drainpipe, which we ripped in half on a table saw.

DIRECTIONS

1 To attach the countertop so it can be removed, if necessary, begin by screwing wooden cleats to the cabinet sides. Make the cleats flush with the top of the cabinets except within the sink compartment. There, screw cleats so their top edge is down ¾ inch plus the thickness of the sink's top edge.

2 Cut ¾-inch-thick plywood to fit within the sink cabinet. Also cut out the sink opening using the template included with the sink. Make the cutout about ¼ inch bigger in all directions if the sink has a bevel and you want it to show. Lower the plywood and the sink into place.

3 Cut the cement-board base (see page 65). But keep the sink cutout about 1 inch back from the eventual edge. If you need to divide the countertop into sections, locate divisions over solid supports. Butt sheets of concrete board there.

4 Drill faucet holes with an abrasive-tipped hole saw in a drill. Faucet holes typically are 1⅜ inches in diameter, but check the size specified for your fittings. Make plugs from short pieces of 1-inch pipe, which has an outside diameter of 1⅜ inches. To make the pipe easier to remove once the concrete is hard, cut a vertical slit and stuff it with something you can pull loose. We used a jigsaw blade.

5 To create an expansion gap, wedge a thin piece of metal between pieces of cement board. We used stainless steel 1½ inches deep and ⅛ inch thick, which we purchased at a metal-supply company for less than $5. We shaped the front edge into a bullnose on a grinding wheel.

1–2

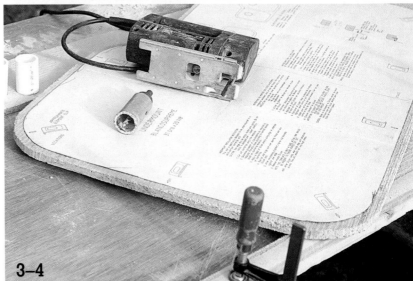

3–4

5

6 Trace the sink template onto 1½-inch-thick foam insulation and cut it out with a jigsaw or a box knife with the blade fully extended. Sand edges and cover with plastic tape. Also cut foam to fit snugly in the bowls. Smooth painter's tape around the top edges of the bowls. If there is a bevel, fill it with plasticine clay. Seal the edge between the sink and the cement board with a bead of caulk.

7 Screw the cement board to the cleats. Next to the sink, where you couldn't fit a screwdriver to loosen the cleats, use machine screws with wing nuts underneath. Cover joints, except at expansion gaps, with mesh tape.

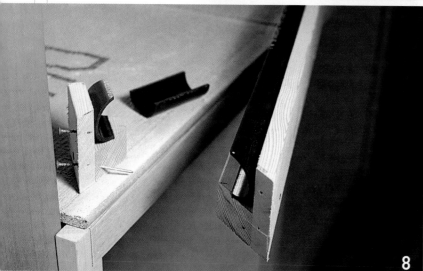

8 Build the edge form. For a bullnose edge, rip a length of 1½-inch drainpipe on a table saw, using a featherboard to hold the pipe firmly to the fence. Build a wooden cradle for the pipe using a 1 by 3 for the vertical piece and a 2 by 2 for the base. Cut out part of the 2 by 2 so the pipe sits into it without leaving a lip. Clamp the cradle to the cabinets so the interior of the bullnose is flush with the bottom of the cement board.

9 Cut expanded-metal lath to fit within the form, staying 1 inch back from all edges. Reinforce skinny sections along the sink with thin mesh strips.

10 With the bowl forms snugged into place, carefully align the larger foam piece and screw the layers together. To keep the foam from lifting when you add the concrete mix, wedge pieces of wood between the foam and the ceiling using small pieces of wood at either end so you don't mar the ceiling or dig into the foam.

11 Plan how you will screed, or level, the concrete. You can run a board back and forth between the front edging and a guide board next to the wall at the back, but the front edge will wind up with a stepped-down edge because of the thickness of the pipe. For a smooth edge, screw the back guide board to the wall and notch the screed so its ends ride along the guide and the pipe and its middle section hangs down and smooths the surface. Work the screed forward in short motions, not side to side.

12 With a spray bottle, thoroughly dampen the cement board.

13 Prepare Basic Sand Mix, page 33, or a bagged sand mix. Then smooth some over the mesh tape. Spread about a ½-inch layer over the counter and pack the front edge thoroughly. Tamp the front edge with a hammer to release air bubbles.

14 Carefully lower the metal lath into place and finish filling the form. Screed it level.

15 Wait a little while and then smooth the surface with a wooden float. Wait a little longer and go over it again with a trowel. See page 38 for tips on achieving a smooth finish.

16 When the concrete stiffens, cover it with plastic and keep it damp for three days before removing the edge form and the foam pieces. Remove any rough spots with either a sanding sponge or a diamond pad.

17 Cut out the foam plugs in the sink. Fill any holes along the sink or front edges with a paste of water and cement tinted to match. To smooth the bullnose patches, rub along the edge with a piece of plastic wrap or a sandwich bag.

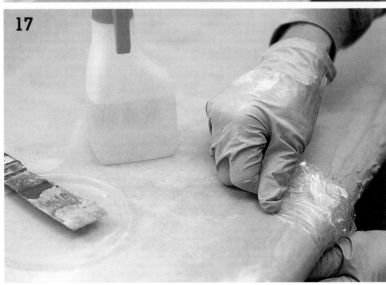

18 Scrub away any concrete traces that seeped onto the sink. Polish the top with fine sandpaper or diamond polishing pads, starting with 120 grit if you want a terrazzo look and 220 if you want more of a troweled finish. Seal and wax the counter before you use it.

OPPOSITE: *Cast with a sinuous curve down the middle, this concrete sink is loaded with special features, including an integral drainboard and a metal grate that slides on a lip cast into the countertop. The basins have metal inlays on the bottom to guard against chipping. The metal is level with the surrounding concrete, so the surface is easy to clean.*

LEFT: *Dual sinks cast into a long countertop create a seamless surface that's easy to keep clean, while the matching multipart backsplash adds interesting detail in this bathroom. Because units such as this are almost always custom made, it's easy to order them in dimensions that fit rooms precisely or accommodate existing plumbing.*

BELOW: *The essence of simplicity, this small vessel sink seems almost jadelike.*

BOTTOM: *Paired with a designer faucet styled to look like a bamboo fountain, this elegant vessel sink sets an Asian theme for this powder room.*

Sinks

LOOKING AS THOUGH THEY WERE CARVED FROM STONE, concrete sinks definitely make a design statement. That statement can range from high-style sleek to farmhouse practical, depending on the sink's style and surroundings. Because concrete has a tendency to chip when knocked with heavy pots, concrete sinks work best in powder rooms or other places where they aren't heavily used. They're also spectacular in outdoor kitchens, potting sheds, and the like, where a few chips just add to the rustic appeal. If you do opt for putting one in your kitchen, consider installing a metal inlay on the bottom in order to help absorb any blows.

ABOVE: *Angular and no-nonsense, a ramp sink and integral counter-top look high-tech and modern. Water drains through a slit at the bottom.*

LEFT: *With faucets at both ends, an unusually long bathroom sink offers all the advantages of the two-sink setup that's common in master bathrooms. But with this sink, you're never cramped. There is plenty of room to hand-wash delicate clothing or even to bathe a puppy.*

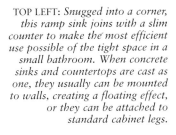

TOP LEFT: *Snugged into a corner, this ramp sink joins with a slim counter to make the most efficient use possible of the tight space in a small bathroom. When concrete sinks and countertops are cast as one, they usually can be mounted to walls, creating a floating effect, or they can be attached to standard cabinet legs.*

TOP RIGHT: *Known as a wave sink, this design merges sink and countertop and helps ensure that all the water goes down the drain. It's available with lots of waves—up to five sinks cast into a single countertop, a setup most in demand in commercial settings.*

BOTTOM RIGHT: *Cast into a countertop with a built-in drainboard, this sink pairs with a matching backsplash. To create the marbleized look, the manufacturer placed handfuls of sand mix into the mold, leaving slight gaps between clumps. Later, those gaps were plugged with a cement putty tinted a darker shade.*

A photograph of an antique sink made of French limestone was the design inspiration for this sink. Besides creating an ideal shape for a garden sink or a potting bench, this "farm style" sink has several practical benefits: the bowls are deep and wide and the apron lines up with the front of cabinets so you don't have to reach as far to use the sink. This means you're less likely to feel back pain.

A farm sink

Building a concrete farm sink is one of the more ambitious projects in this book. You'll need to make two forms—one to shape the inside surface, the other to establish the exterior. You'll also need to fashion a wire cage to slip between the forms as reinforcing to keep the corners from cracking.

DIRECTIONS

1 Begin the form for the sink interior by outlining the inside of the rim on foam insulation. Cut around the edges with a box cutter with its blade fully extended or with a fine-tooth saw, such as a band saw or jigsaw. Copy the shape to make enough layers for the depth of the sink. Here we used four layers of 2-inch-thick foam and made the sink 21 inches long and $14\frac{1}{2}$ inches wide.

2 Dribble a little wood glue onto the sheets and then screw them together with a few long screws. We used screws sold for holding landscaping timbers together. (When the glue has dried, you can remove the screws and cut through the layers in a V, as shown, to make it easier to remove the foam from the cast concrete. Use the same screws to tie the pieces back together.) With a rasp, round over the foam edge that will shape the bottom of the sink.

3 Coat the foam with drywall joint compound (the standard type, not fast-setting). Don't worry if it looks a bit messy. Form a slight mountain on the base of the form so that when the sink is cast in reverse the concrete will slope toward a drain at the center.

4 After the joint compound has dried, remove bulges with a sanding sponge or sandpaper. Fill divots with joint compound and repeat the drying and sanding steps.

5 From foam insulation, cut a plug to fit snugly into the basket of the sink drain. Screw this to the base of the mold.

6 Brush dust off the mold and paint with two coats of shellac.

81

7 Build an open box of melamine-coated particleboard to form the sink exterior, which is 2 inches bigger in all directions than the interior form. With a hole saw in a drill, cut into the base to accommodate the pipe section of the sink strainer.

8 Make a wire cage to reinforce the sink. Bend sections of ¼- or ½-inch threaded rod to make a top rim 1 inch bigger in all directions than the interior mold. Lash overlaps together with 20-gauge wire. Cut ½-inch galvanized hardware cloth to form a sink shape. Make the base 2 inches shorter and narrower than the exterior mold. Fold up flaps for the ends and sides, which need to be 4 inches shorter than the interior mold's sides. Leave an extra inch or two on the hardware cloth so that you can fold the top edge over the rim of threaded rod. Stitch all of this together with 20-gauge wire. Cut a hole in the bottom of the cage so that it fits over the sink strainer.

9 Screw three short 2 by 4s to the base of the exterior mold. Locate the middle 2 by 4 so that the drainpipe hits it. Drill a shallow recess into the 2 by 4 for the drainpipe. Make the recess just deep enough so that the rim of the sink strainer sits 2 inches above the base of the sink. Screw the strainer to the wood through the strainer's center hole. Smooth plasticine clay around the form's corners so that the sink's exterior will have rounded edges.

10 Spread a thin band of nonhardening plasticine clay around the rim of the sink strainer to preserve space for plumber's putty when you install the sink. Press down the clay and make it as even as possible. Trim the edge with a pottery tool or knife. Then coat the exterior of the strainer with wax and cover the top edge with plastic wrap and the lid of a large yogurt container or similar cover.

11 Prepare Basic Sand Mix, page 33, or a bagged sand mix. Use concrete bonding adhesive for half the water unless the sand mix label says to use only water. On a sturdy, level work surface, place the exterior form on three or four dowels spaced so that you can rock the mold back and forth as you fill it. Spread about ½ inch of the mix into the bottom of the mold.

12 Roll the form back and forth to work out air bubbles. Stop when you see the sand mix settle and water just beginning to rise. Add another ½ inch of the sand mix and rock again.

13 Lower the wire cage into place and fill with another inch of sand mix. Rock. Then add more sand mix and trowel smooth so that the filling reaches just to the top of the drain.

14 Remove covers on the top of the drain. Lower the interior form into place and screw and clamp two boards across the top. Fill the sides with sand mix. Stop every inch or so to roll the form back and forth and to tamp down the mix with a dowel. Tap sides with a hammer.

15 Smooth the top edge with a putty knife. When the sand mix stiffens, most likely within a few hours, remove the wooden braces to get access to the entire top rim. Clean up any rough spots with the putty knife.

16 Wait three days. Then remove the interior mold by cutting through the foam with a box knife. Use a small pry bar to loosen layers. Don't pry against the sink itself, however.

17 Fill any holes with a paste of cement and water tinted to match the sink. Rub off any excess. When the paste is dry, apply a sealer to the sink.

11

12

13

14

Mantles, hearths, and fireplace surrounds

CONCRETE ABSORBS AND HOLDS HEAT but does not burn, making it a terrific material for mantles and fireplace surrounds. The flush-front gas and electric fireplaces common today sometimes seem like just part of the cabinetry, but with a concrete mantle or surround they become focal points. If you enjoy cozying up to a fire, consider adding an elevated hearth, which is also easy to execute in concrete. If you continue the hearth to a nearby wall, it will double as a seating ledge and a convenient place to set down books or trays of snacks.

BELOW: *A rough-hewn lintel made of natural stone contrasts with the smooth texture of the concrete surround and mantle.*

OPPOSITE, TOP: *Glazed tiles painted with an olive motif decorate this substantial fireplace surround, designed in a simple but classic style similar to that of fireplaces carved from stone.*

LEFT: *With its molded edge, this concrete mantle carries out the "European country" theme of the house. It also serves a practical purpose by wrapping around the corner to provide extra display space.*

BELOW: *When the fire's going, the raised hearth of this imposing fireplace becomes one of the coziest spots in the house. With a raised hearth, debris from a fire is less likely to spread across the floor, and you don't have to bend over as much to tend the fire.*

NEAR RIGHT: *Mitered like a picture frame, this fireplace surround helps create a somewhat formal tone in this room.*

FAR RIGHT: *This fireplace serves as a focal point in more ways than one. Above the concrete surround and mantle a television is tucked into a cabinet with doors that are normally kept closed.*

ABOVE: *This expansive hearth anchors an island wall that separates the living room from the music room. It also connects the fireplace and the wood storage area, provides spillover seating for guests, and works as a display area.*

RIGHT: *Although concrete surrounds often create a sense of mass, they also can look relatively petite, as this one does. It's important to match the size and style of a surround to the scale of the room.*

OPPOSITE, BOTTOM: *Similar in design to the fireplace shown at right, this surround nevertheless has a more massive look. The firebox is elevated and the mantle is thicker.*

Cast in three parts so it would be easy to carry and lift into place, this concrete mantle shows off one of the homeowners' hobbies: collecting fossils, petrified wood, and other interesting rocks.

A mantle with carving and inlays

We placed the inlays along the front edge as each mold was filled with a stiff sand-and-cement mixture, tucking the mix around the rocks so that they were completely embedded. Then we troweled the top of the concrete mixture and waited for it to stiffen. After removing the sides of the molds, we carved out some of the concrete along the front edge to reveal the inlays.

Because we cast the pieces right side up in a mold, no complicated "upside down" thinking was needed to visualize how the front edge would turn out. The finished mantle shows exactly the way the pieces of rock were placed and the effect created by carving out the excess concrete mix.

DIRECTIONS

1 Build molds from melamine-coated particleboard or plywood. Our molds consisted of three open-top boxes. They lined up to create sections that span the mantle plus short overlaps where pieces meet. (For clarity, the mold ends are shown here opposite the finished pieces.) To create the bottom recess, which fits over the fireplace bricks, we inserted a board toward the back of the mold.

2 Gather decorative materials and arrange them on a surface marked to show the dimensions of the finished mantle edge. When you are satisfied with the arrangement, seal areas that you will expose so that concrete doesn't cloud the surface. We used shellac as a sealer. It dries in about a half-hour.

3 Prepare a Basic Sand Mix, page 33, or a bagged sand mix, keeping it on the dry side. Working from one end of the mold, place the rocks vertically into position and pack sand mix around them. Embed the rocks completely. Then fill the rest of the form. Level the mixture and trowel it smooth, as shown on pages 37 and 38.

4 Wait one hour or several hours until the sand mix becomes firm. Remove screws from the outside of the molds but leave the base pieces in place. Carve into the edge to expose the rocks and add detail, as you wish. Brush the inlays free of debris.

5 Cover the pieces with plastic and wait at least three days. Polish the top with fine wet-dry sandpaper. Clean the concrete and let it dry. Seal if you wish. We rubbed the top with wax and buffed it to a sheen.

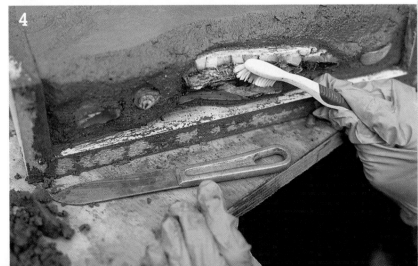

Floors

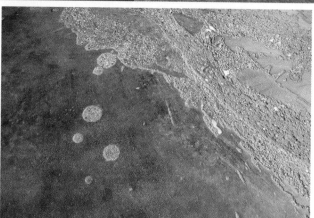

NOT TOO LONG AGO, IF YOU HAD A CONCRETE FLOOR, chances are you covered it up with tile, linoleum, carpet, or wood—anything to hide that ugly gray. That's no longer the case. Today, thanks to acid stains, paints, stamps, and other products, as well as a growing awareness of how to use them, concrete floors can be works of art. If you're planning a new house or an addition, choosing a decorative concrete floor will probably save you money because you won't need any other finished flooring. If you have an existing house, a wide array of topping mixtures, some of which need to be only 1/8 inch thick, allow you to create a decorative concrete floor over whatever subfloor you have.

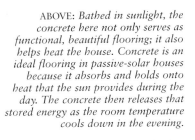

ABOVE: *Bathed in sunlight, the concrete here not only serves as functional, beautiful flooring; it also helps heat the house. Concrete is an ideal flooring in passive-solar houses because it absorbs and holds onto heat that the sun provides during the day. The concrete then releases that stored energy as the room temperature cools down in the evening.*

RIGHT: *Johnny Grey, a kitchen designer from England, included Chippendale-style cabinets and sweeping curves in this kitchen. Custom-made cement-body floor tiles in contrasting colors and shapes add to the distinctive look. The tiles, each up to 30 inches square, look a bit like marble because of the way the concrete was placed into the molds a handful at a time.*

OPPOSITE, TOP: *A concrete floor pulls together the elements of this easy-care living room, which also features a built-in concrete bench, a concrete fireplace surround, and a concrete coffee table. They contrast beautifully with the bright walls and the glowing amber of natural wood.*

OPPOSITE, MIDDLE: *Aiming to mimic the look of a beach, the contractor who created this unusual floor incorporated aquarium sands and seashells. He also applied several colors of acid stains.*

OPPOSITE, BOTTOM: *Buff and copper acid stains create the mottled color on this floor.*

ABOVE LEFT: *Because pigments that stand up to the alkalinity of cement tend to be somewhat muted and the designers of this floor wanted vivid color, they opted to paint the design. Water-based paints work best for painting floors.*

ABOVE RIGHT: *A ⅛-inch layer of gray polymer-modified concrete was applied over an old concrete floor. The next day, acid stain in a color known as Aged Buff was rubbed in. Two coats of sealer and two of wax produced the sheen.*

OPPOSITE: *Thinned, naturally pigmented linseed oil–based paints add a warm look to this concrete floor.*

BOTTOM RIGHT: *This floor was topped with a cement-acrylic mixture, then troweled and burnished. Powdered mica was scattered on the topping as it was being troweled.*

BELOW: *Looking very much like handmade Saltillo tiles, the main expanse of this concrete floor was created by cutting a grid and staining the squares with several tones of acid stain. After the stain dried, the grid lines were filled with grout.*

Most of the concrete floors shown in this book were poured when the house was built. But it's possible to create similar designs on existing floors by using a cementitious coating. Some manufacturers recommend using their toppings only over concrete subfloors, but the product we chose, Rotofino, from Colormaker Floors, can also be used

A decorative cement floor topping

over wood subfloors. The trick is to first install a layer of $\frac{1}{2}$-inch Hardiplank, a type of cement board, which stiffens the floor and provides a cement-based substrate so the coating can bond properly. Taping the joints should prevent gaps between the cement board from showing in the finished floor, but you still want to design your floor with lines that follow these joints. That way, if cracks do develop, they will look like part of your design.

DIRECTIONS

1 Assemble the needed tools: a $\frac{1}{2}$-inch drill (can be rented) with a paddle mixer and a 5-gallon bucket; homemade knee boards (shown) with only screw tips protruding on the back so that you can work on the coating to trowel it; a floor gauge roller with $\frac{1}{16}$-inch-deep ridges; and a pool trowel, which has rounded ends.

2 Screw $\frac{1}{2}$-inch-thick Hardiplank panels to the subfloor, using one screw at each mark on the panel. Cover seams with mesh tape and trowel a thinset mortar (we used Slimpatch™ from the L. M. Scofield Company) over the tape, as if you were covering joints in drywall.

3 The next day, when the patches are dry, use a garden sprayer to apply the primer, as recommended by the manufacturer. Use two coats if that is recommended.

4 Prepare the coating as the label specifies. Working from a back corner toward a doorway in sections small enough so that you can reach across them, pour on a few cupfuls of the coating and immediately smooth out the product with the floor gauge roller. Work quickly.

5 Allow the coating to stiffen, then trowel smooth with the pool trowel. Work on the knee boards, smoothing over your tracks as you back out of the room.

6 The next day, decorate the coating. Score a grid with an angle grinder (wear a mask and goggles), then mist on two coats of acid stain. Rub in the first coat with a sponge and the second with a rag. Acid stains look clear at first. The color develops over an hour or so.

7 Neutralize the acid with an alkali as the manufacturer recommends. Rinse with water a few times and remove with a shop vac until the water is clear. Allow to dry. Seal and wax.

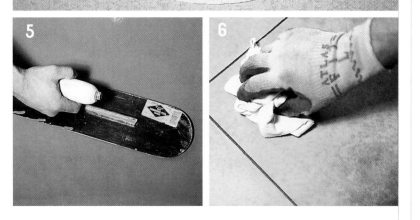

Paths and patios

CONCRETE PATHS AND PATIOS often mimic natural stone. They can also have a look all their own. Consider finishes used on interior floors, provided the surfaces aren't too slick. Or opt for treatments, such as exposed aggregate, that typically are used only outdoors.

Big expanses of paving are probably best left to professionals, but smaller-scale paths or patios make good projects for people with only a little experience building with concrete. The smaller the pour, the better. If this is your introduction to this material, a project such as the steppingstone path, on page 100, is an ideal place to start.

OPPOSITE, TOP: *Large, individually cast pavers create an inviting courtyard that looks striking because of the interplay of stone sizes. To create a project like this without having to lift the heavy pavers, pour alternate sections and then fill in between them, as shown in the project that begins on page 104.*

OPPOSITE, MIDDLE: *Like a carpet under a dining table, a grid of rectangles and diamonds sets off this patio dining area.*

OPPOSITE, BOTTOM: *This used to be an old, cracked concrete driveway. Using a 4-inch angle grinder, a concrete artist first cut random lines, then applied acid stains.*

RIGHT: *Contractors who specialize in decorative concrete use pigments and either stamps or paper stencils with textured rollers to produce surfaces that resemble slate or other stone.*

BELOW: *This pathway and driveway started out as ordinary concrete. A topping of polymer concrete was added and the flagstone design was stamped in.*

ABOVE: *Smooth concrete tinted with several tones of acid stains enrich this walkway and patio. The ball decorations along the edges are also made of concrete and were cast in molds sold for this purpose.*

LEFT: *Pillow-shaped concrete pavers tinted in slightly different shades help give this California patio an Old World look. The owner devised the technique as a less expensive alternative to importing stone paving from Europe.*

OPPOSITE, TOP: *Diamond-shape pavers create a fun harlequin look at this urban residence.*

OPPOSITE, BOTTOM: *The builders of this house have Italian roots and love Italian architecture, so they tried to incorporate key features in the design of this New World home. A bare concrete patio just would not do; they outlined borders by cutting around the edge and the center. Then they colored the design with acid stains and added a birdbath to complete the look.*

By casting individual steppingstones, you can create a one-of-a-kind pathway without having to deal with a large quantity of concrete all at once. Each concrete batch is small, so you should have plenty of time to add pebble mosaics or other decorations, even if you work alone.

A steppingstone path

Although the shape of these steppingstones is complex, the mold is easy to build. Create the curved shape by cutting a plywood base and then attaching strips of aluminum or galvanized-steel flashing around the edges. We used a kidney shape, so the back of one piece interlocks with the front of the next piece. This allows you to place the steppingstones close together to create a solid walkway if you wish.

With our shape, one 60-pound bag of sand mix was more than enough to fill the mold. We measured the amount left over and reduced the dry ingredients by a little less than that on subsequent pours.

DIRECTIONS

1 Sketch the shape on newspaper and transfer it to ¾-inch plywood. Our design is 25 inches long and about 14 inches wide. Cut along the line with a jigsaw.

2 For a mold 2 inches deep, cut aluminum or galvanized-steel flashing into a strip 2¾ inches wide and long enough to go around the mold with a little excess. (Measure the perimeter with string.) To cut the metal without creating ripples, score it several times with a utility knife. Then fold the sheet back and forth against a straightedge. If the flashing is thin, cut two strips and sandwich them together with plastic tape, as we did. Nail the bottom of the strip or strips to the plywood; use screws on inward curves so you can release the edging later.

3 Spray the base with shellac to reduce the amount of moisture the plywood will absorb. When the shellac dries, spray all interior mold surfaces with cooking oil. Blot with a paper towel. Screw short pieces of wood to the ends of the form so you have handles to help you remove the mold.

Tip

YOU CAN ALSO USE THIS TECHNIQUE to build molds for countertops, tabletops, and other curved projects.

4. Prepare Basic Sand Mix, page 33, or a bagged sand mix. Fill the mold with it. Begin decorating immediately. Outline shapes, if you wish, by lightly pressing cookie cutter patterns made of flashing into the surface. Dampen pebbles and place them into the sand mix vertically. Submerge most of each piece. As you complete a section, cover the stones with a small piece of plywood and, using a hammer, tamp them nearly flush with the surface. If your design includes large and small stones, place and tamp large ones first; then add the small pieces and tamp again.

5. With a trowel, embed all the stones securely by working the surface cream of cement and fine sand between the pieces. It's fine to cover the stones completely with the sand mix.

6. Wait several hours, until the sand mix stiffens. Then brush off the surface to reveal the pebbles. If the concrete is still rather soft, use a nylon brush and wipe the surface with a sponge that's been well wrung out. If the concrete is hard, use a metal brush and rinse with a fine spray of water.

7. In one to two days, remove the steppingstone from the mold. Loosen screws on inward curves and break the seal around the top edge with a putty knife. Invert, resting the handles on scraps of wood so the steppingstone can drop out. If gravity isn't enough, tap the form with a mallet.

8. Round over the edge with a stiff, sharp-edged tool. A painter's 5-in-1 tool works well.

9 Establish the route of your path with a hose, then set steppingstones in place. If you want them one stride apart, walk across the lawn and mark your footprints. Or establish a set stride length and subtract the width of one steppingstone. Cut a spacer block to match the remaining distances. Our pieces are 8 inches apart (on the outside of the curve).

10 To set a steppingstone into a lawn without creating a mess, hammer a 2-inch-wide brick chisel straight down around the edge of the concrete. Remove the steppingstone and use gloved hands or a small shovel to separate the root wads in the sod from the underlying soil. Roll back the sod and remove.

11 Smooth a layer of sand across the hole, then tip the steppingstone in place. Jiggle it back and forth until it feels level and solid.

Tip

IF A STEPPINGSTONE STILL WOBBLES after you set it on sand, remove the piece, take out a handful of sand at the center of the hole, and replace the steppingstone. Press and wiggle it until you have seated it firmly.

Pouring a path in place allows you to build a wide expanse of weed-free paving without having to carry or level the finished pieces. This pathway was designed for a family that wanted a folk theme. Because they raise chickens, the design evolved to include feather inlays (cut from copper) and a texture created by pressing chicken wire into the surface as it stiffened.

A path that's poured in place

feather inlays (cut from copper) and a texture created by pressing chicken wire into the surface as it stiffened.

This 4-inch-thick path is 9$\frac{1}{2}$ feet long and varies in width from 2 feet to 6$\frac{1}{2}$ feet, too small to have concrete delivered from a truck and too large for a few people to mix and pour concrete all at once. So the path was poured in stages: first the ends, then the middle. We used a 3.5-cubic-foot mixer, sold at home centers.

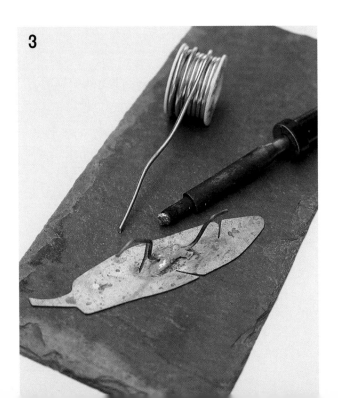

Tip

YOU CAN ALSO CREATE a patio using this method. Build forms in a checkerboard and pour alternate sections. Then go back and pour the rest. If you use rot-resistant material for the forms, you can leave them in place as part of your design.

DIRECTIONS

1 Excavate the area, spread gravel, and build a form, as shown on page 20. Tamp the gravel base thoroughly. Use a motorized tamper (before you add the forms) if you have a large space or a hand tamper, as shown here, if you have a small space.

2 With aviator's snips or another suitable tool, cut pieces of chicken wire to fit within each section, minus a 2-inch perimeter. Remove the wire and place it on the lawn or on another flat area. Weight the wire so it straightens.

3 Make feather inlays or other designs from copper sheeting, which cuts almost as easily as wood. Wearing goggles, use a scroll saw or a coping saw with a fine-tooth blade. File edges. Solder wire strands to the backs to anchor the inlays to the concrete. Clean off flux residue.

4 Prepare Basic Concrete Mix, page 33, or a bagged mix (with ½ gallon extra cement per bag if you use a standard mix). You'll need several batches to fill each section of a path this size. Dump each batch into the form and spread with a rake. Tamp thoroughly when the section is full.

5 Run a straight 2 by 4 back and forth across the form to screed, or level, the concrete.

6 Run an edging tool around the perimeter. If rocks get in the way, first smooth the edge by pressing straight down with a margin trowel. Don't attempt to make the edge perfectly smooth at this point; your main goal is to push down any rocks that are near the surface.

7 Allow the concrete to set a little. Then smooth the section with a trowel.

8 Embed the feather inlays. Press them down into the concrete and wiggle them gently to help the concrete fill in around the anchor wires. It's better to seat inlays a bit too deep than to risk having them sit above the surface, where an edge might lift up.

9 When the surface is somewhat stiff but still pliable, carefully set the chicken wire in place. With a trowel in each hand, transfer the design by pressing straight down. Vary the pressure if you want a variegated surface, as we did. Don't attempt to trowel in a circular motion; your tool will snag on the wire. Lift the wire and smooth the perimeter with the edging tool again.

10 As the concrete hardens, clean excess concrete from the inlay surface with a sponge.

11 Keep the concrete damp for at least three days. Then remove the perimeter forms.

Tip

TO KEEP CONCRETE damp in dry weather, cover it with plastic or cardboard and mist it several times a day. Or apply a curing compound. Pigment manufacturers recommend using these compounds on tinted concrete to prevent stains that can appear if the concrete dries unevenly.

8

9

10

Furniture

CONCRETE FURNITURE RANGES from simple benches and tabletops to complex barbecue setups. In a sunroom or family room, a tabletop made of concrete sets the tone for casual elegance. Outdoors, concrete benches, chairs, and tables serve double duty, providing both practicality and garden decoration. The concrete gradually weathers to resemble valuable antiques carved from stone.

There are several practical details to deal with before you buy or build concrete furniture. First, consider the weight. A concrete tabletop will need to remain where you install it. So will concrete seating, unless it's made from special lightweight mixes. A firm footing, such as a poured concrete pad, is needed for tables or heavy pedestals so they don't sink or tip. And remember that concrete benches can be hard. Provide cushions if you want your guests to linger.

ABOVE: *A polished slab of concrete made with bits of recycled Chardonnay bottles as the aggregate serves as an easy-care tabletop in this dining room.*

OPPOSITE, BOTTOM: *The glass top on this table invites visitors to contemplate the forces that hold together parts of the base, which is made of a lightweight concrete called Syndesis.*

BELOW: *This three-piece lounging bench interlocks in a way that helps keep the pieces aligned.*

NEAR RIGHT: *Mounted to a wall, a simple box made of concrete works well in an entry as a catchall for wet umbrellas, keys, and other items.*

FAR RIGHT: *Made from light-weight Syndesis concrete, this table and bench add to the easygoing ambiance of a dining area. The floor is also concrete, so the benches slide easily when it's time to clean up.*

FAR LEFT: *Cast upside down in a mold, this desktop looks striking in part because of its intricate edge pattern. Creating the mold for the design was easy: the builder merely tacked wood molding into the form walls.*

NEAR LEFT: *Pieces of broken pottery inlay the edges of this 16-foot-long concrete table, set in a garden filled with artistic touches brought back from the designer's global travels. The table seats 12 but is often used as a roomy buffet table.*

OPPOSITE, TOP: *Concrete furniture isn't something you move around on a whim. It tends to stay where it is—like this table, which was built to encircle the tree at the center.*

RIGHT: *In a house with concrete floors, this concrete table fits right in. It's used for everything from paying bills to eating a quick meal.*

BELOW: *This free-form mosaic tabletop reflects the sunny mood of the rest of the well-lighted room. An artist glued broken pieces of tile to a base surrounded by a metal band and then filled in around the tiles with a concrete patch product usually used to fill cracks in driveways.*

Created in three parts, this garden bench is spacious enough for two people to share a view or pause to chat. The seat, cast with two recesses underneath, slips into place over rebar stubs that protrude from the legs. Both the seat and the legs include decorative features. The top was lightly dusted with white cement and then colored

A garden bench

with two tones of acid stain, Padre Brown and Antique Bronze. That produced a richly aged look. The edges are ragged, reminiscent of rough-hewn stone, but the top edge is rounded over for comfort. The legs boast a rippled edge, created by slipping short pieces of metal roofing into the form.

DIRECTIONS

1 Create a decorative edge for the legs with strips of metal roofing. Cut two pieces 6 inches wide using a circular saw with a metal roofing blade or a plywood blade attached backward. To guide the saw, screw a straightedge to plywood and clamp this assembly over the roofing, which should be supported with pieces of 2 by 4 on sawhorses. Wear goggles and ear protection—you'll see sparks and hear a screech.

2 Build the form for the legs. Then draw a cut-off triangle on a 2-foot-square piece of melamine-coated particleboard; make the shape 16 inches high, 15 inches wide at the base, and 7 inches wide at the top. Extend lines around to the back so you know where to locate screws. Cut edge pieces 6 inches wide and bevel the ends to match your drawing. Cut the top and bottom pieces so they reach past the sides. In the top piece, drill a ½-inch hole, centered. Screw the sides to the base and then screw the top and bottom to the sides. With tin snips, cut the roofing strips to fit. Slide them into place.

3 Spray the interior with cooking oil. Prepare Basic Concrete Mix, page 33, or a bagged mix (with ½ gallon extra cement if you use a standard mix). One 80-pound bag of high-strength concrete mix is the perfect amount. Fill the form halfway. Mark a 6-inch stub of rebar ⅝ inch from one end with easy-to-see blue painter's tape. Slip the rebar through the hole in the top and adjust the bar so the mark lines up with the inside of the form. Finish filling the form and trowel the surface smooth. After a day or two, unscrew the top and bottom and tip the concrete out of the form. Pull off the metal, clean the form of excess concrete, and spray the mold with cooking oil before refilling for the second leg.

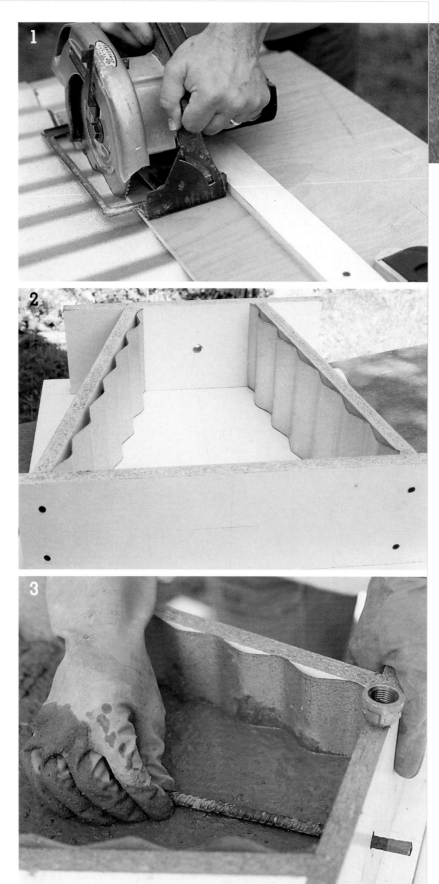

113

4 Cut pieces for the bench-seat form by making an open box from melamine-coated particleboard. The base is 15 inches wide and 48 inches long, ringed by side pieces that are 3¼ inches wide (to produce a seat 2½ inches thick).

5 Line the side pieces with potter's clay before you attach them to the base. Slice off pieces of clay with wire and roll flat. Cut off a ¾-inch-wide strip along one edge so the base piece can slide underneath.

6 Screw the sides to the base and to each other at the corners. Press a broken brick into the clay, working your way around the form. Then, with a potter's cutting tool, carve a rounded edge into the clay along the base. This creates the mold for a snag-free edge along the top of the seat.

7 Spray the clay with cooking oil and lightly mist oil onto the base of the mold. Wipe all the excess from the melamine. If you wish, sift a few drifts of white cement over the bottom of the mold. This will create a "Milky Way" look on the final piece. Or, if you coat the concrete with acid stains, as we did, it will add to the color variation.

Tip

IF YOU CONSTRUCT a one-person bench, about 30 inches long, you can omit the rebar.

8 Prepare another batch of concrete mix, enough to fill the bench-top form. Place it in the form one handful at a time, creating a layer that is about ½ inch thick. Tamp out air bubbles. With a hammer, beat on the form from underneath. You should see bubbles rise. Stop when a water glaze covers the surface.

9 Continue filling the form, stopping periodically to tap the sides with a hammer. When the form is full and you're finished tapping, level the surface with a 2 by 4. Place three pieces of ³⁄₈-inch rebar lengthwise, 1 inch from each side and down the middle. Tap them down as shown on page 117. Smooth over the surface with a trowel. To create recesses to hold the rebar stubs on the legs, fill two pipe caps with clay and stick them to pieces of plastic. Wiggle the caps down into the concrete about 9 inches from each end, keeping the plastic flush with the surface.

10 Cover and allow to cure for at least two days, then remove the form. Fill any holes with a paste of cement, pigment, and water. Allow the seat to dry slowly in shade.

11 When the seat is at least two weeks old, apply acid stain. Following all safety instructions from the manufacturer, brush on the watery solution and wait for vivid color to develop. Neutralize any remaining stain with baking soda. Scrub away residue with handfuls of sawdust. Rinse thoroughly.

With a few simple adjustments, you can turn the bench project on page 112 into one that results in a table. The legs are the same as those for the bench, except that you need four and must cast a length of pipe down the middle of each one, rather than insert the rebar stub. When you have made all the parts, you can invert two legs on top of the others, thread rebar through the pipes to pin the leg pieces together, and, presto, the bench structure rises to table height. A nub of rebar that protrudes from each leg holds the tabletop in place.

A concrete table

We cast the top right side up and troweled the surface smooth before pressing on vine maple leaves dusted with pigment and cement. This table is heavy. Make sure you have a stable base.

DIRECTIONS

1 Build a leg form like the one on page 113, but drill ⁵⁄₈-inch holes in the top and bottom for a dowel that temporarily holds up a ¹⁄₂-inch plastic pipe cut to the leg's height. Copying the bench leg exactly results in a table 32½ inches high—4 inches taller than most dining tables but a good height for a potting bench or other work surface. Adjust the height if you wish.

2 Build an open box to mold the tabletop. Ours is 24 inches wide and 49 inches long. The mold sides are 3¼ inches deep, producing a top 2½ inches thick. For a shaped edge, nail mitered molding to the sides. Create recesses for the rebar, as shown in Step 9 on page 115. Prepare Basic Concrete Mix, page 33, or a bagged concrete mix (with ½ gallon extra cement if you use a standard mix). Pour the concrete, pound under and around the form with a hammer, and screed the surface. Then place four pieces of ³⁄₈-inch-thick rebar (cut 2 inches shorter than the top) onto the concrete. Equally space the pieces, starting 1 inch from the sides. With a marked stick and a hammer, tap the rebar 1 inch deep. Smooth the surface with a trowel. Slightly round over the outer edge with a trowel.

3 Decorate the concrete after all surface water is gone. Mist the veined side of leaves with water. Dust with a mixture of pigment and cement. Place the leaves, pigment side down, on the concrete. Smooth edges so the leaves adhere. Carefully trowel over them. Wipe the trowel if it picks up pigment. Then trowel the entire table-top again. Cover. Peel off the leaves when the concrete is firm. Remove edge forms after about two days. Keep the concrete damp for several more days before you put the table together.

Planters

CONCRETE PLANTERS range from petite pieces perfect for a single orchid to giant urns capable of housing trees. There are several construction methods, shown in the following projects. Some concrete planters stand up to freezing weather while others fall apart as ice crystals form and cause the concrete to crack. The key is the amount of water used in the initial mix. If you add only enough so the cement mixture barely clumps into a ball, the planter should survive in all weather conditions. The pressed pot on page 120 depends on this technique. You can also use this approach for the carved pot (page 126) and the tufa planter (page 122).

BELOW: *Circular concrete shapes resist cracking better than square shapes do, an important consideration if you live where winter temperatures drop below freezing and you plan to keep a planter outdoors all year. Many different shapes qualify as "circular," as this picture shows.*

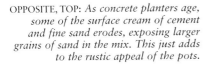

OPPOSITE, TOP: *As concrete planters age, some of the surface cream of cement and fine sand erodes, exposing larger grains of sand in the mix. This just adds to the rustic appeal of the pots.*

ABOVE LEFT: *Although the pot is concrete and the post underneath is natural stone, they pair beautifully, especially because of their lichen glaze.*

ABOVE RIGHT: *Adding artistic elements made of concrete is a great way to turn a garden into a personal retreat. In this garden, the owner placed a large water bowl at the center and added statuary and other garden art around it.*

BOTTOM RIGHT: *Created with layers of colored concrete, this tall planter and base add a sense of height to a garden.*

Create garden pots that rival expensive European antiques by using a round rock to pound a mixture of cement and sand into a sturdy form. Known as "dry-casting," this technique depends on adding only the minimum amount of water. You need to be able

A pressed pot

to get the mixture to clump, but it cannot sag out of shape. Pounding the mixture into the form produces a glorious surface on the molded face, one more like sandstone than concrete. Because the cement never gets wet enough to create a paste, there's little point in adding pigment to this type of project. The sand color predominates. It's worth searching out tan or yellow sand to give your pots a special look. Even fine details of the mold transfer beautifully.

DIRECTIONS

1 Find or build a mold to support the exterior of your planter. If the mold flexes, embed it in sand. We used a 20-inch-wide plastic garden pot and filled part of the base ring with plasticine clay so remaining sections would become feet on the finished pot. For a drain hole, screw through the mold into a short piece of dowel on the interior. Spray with cooking oil and wipe off the excess.

2 Wearing a mask and gloves, combine 2 parts sand and 1 part cement. Incorporate plastic fibers (sold as reinforcing for concrete) if you wish. Work in just enough water so you can squeeze the mixture into a ball. Starting at the bottom, pound handfuls against the mold with a round rock. Aim for a layer about 1 inch thick. For especially large pots, walls can be up to 2 inches thick. Cover the pot and keep it moist.

3 Free the bowl from the mold after two days. Invert the mold and unscrew the drain dowel. Tap the mold with a mallet to free the pot. You may have to hit the mold rather aggressively; aim for the base, not the walls. Remove the drain dowel by drilling through it with an undersize bit; pick out remaining wood with pliers.

4 If the top edge looks ragged, smooth it with a rasp and a sanding sponge. Smooth the interior, if necessary, with the sanding sponge, scrapers, or other tools.

Incorporate peat moss in a mixture of sand and cement and you'll wind up with "hypertufa," a rocklike material that resembles natural tufa stone. Pronounced "toofa," it often develops a crust of moss and lichen, adding to its appeal. Hypertufa planters

A hypertufa planter

make ideal troughs for miniature alpine plants or cacti. Because a rustic appearance is part of the charm, forms for shaping hypertufa can be supersimple. You can use nesting cardboard boxes or mold the material freehand on the outside of an old plastic pot. After several days, the mixture will be hard enough for you to fine-tune the shape with a wire brush or improvised carving tools. Allow hypertufa pots to cure out of direct sunlight for several weeks.

DIRECTIONS

1 Nesting cardboard boxes with a gap of at least 1 inch all around make good molds. Brace the sides with concrete blocks or wood clamped in place. If one box is more rectangular than the other, you can adjust the larger box by screwing pieces of wood inside. We added wood to only the lower portion of opposite walls to create handles. If you want a drain hole, tape a short dowel or a pipe stub to the bottom of the box and oil it well.

2 There are several recipes for hypertufa. A basic one: mix 2 parts sand and 2 parts sifted peat moss with 1 to 1½ cups cement. Or, for a more lightweight mix, substitute perlite (the white component in this mortar tray) for half of the sand. Combine dry ingredients, then add enough water to make a moist but not soggy mix that you can form into clumps.

3 Set the large box on a flat surface where it can remain undisturbed for several days. Fill the bottom with the cement mixture and pack it firmly. Stop when the bottom is as thick as the gap between the two boxes. Insert the smaller box and fill with bags of sand. Press the cement mixture between the walls, tamping as you go. Round over the top edge. Cover with plastic.

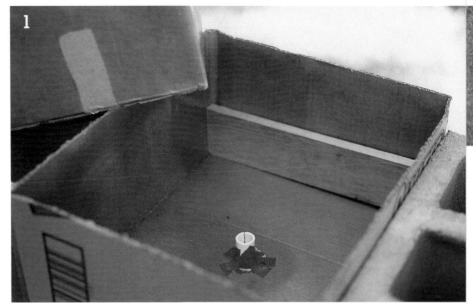

4 Instead of forming hypertufa between two cardboard boxes, you can use a smooth bowl as a form and apply the material by hand to its exterior. Slip a thin plastic bag over the bowl first to make the cast easy to remove. Spread out the plastic and invert the bowl over a sturdy surface where your project can remain undisturbed for several days. Attach the bowl to the work surface with a pad of potter's clay, if you have one.

5 Mix the hypertufa using one of the recipes in Step 2 on page 123. Keep the mixture stiff; add only enough water so you can press the tufa into a ball. Form hamburger-size patties and pat them onto the bowl, aiming for a layer about 1 inch thick. Start at the rim and work up.

6 Shape what will be the bottom of the planter into a concave curve so the pot won't wobble. If you want a drain hole, poke it in now.

Tip

TO NEUTRALIZE THE ALKALINITY of the cement before you plant, immerse your pot in a solution of 1/2 cup vinegar to 1 gallon water for about a half hour. To hasten the growth of moss and algae on the planter, paint it with a mixture of beer and sugar or a mix of butter-milk and pulverized moss.

7 Whether you have shaped your tufa planter with cardboard boxes or with a plastic-covered bowl, wait at least 1½ days for the mixture to firm up; then remove the mold. (If you screwed wood to the cardboard, remove the screws before you pull away the box.)

8 With a wire brush or a rasp, fine-tune the shape and remove telltale signs of the mold, such as ribs from corrugated cardboard or wrinkles from plastic. Because tufa planters are meant to resemble weathered rock, they usually look best with a rough surface. Although the tufa is stiff at this point, it is still rather weak. Handle your planter carefully.

9 You can carve details into your tufa planter if you wish. Consider Mayan designs and other ancient artwork that was executed by chipping into rock. As with any project made with cement, the longer you keep your planter damp, the stronger it will become. Keep it covered for at least several more days and out of the sun for several weeks.

It's very easy to carve cement mixtures when they are set but not yet very strong. If you try to remove a garden pot from a typical mold at this point, however, the bowl is likely to crumble. This project features a mold system that's easy to remove so you can

A carved pot

begin carving as soon as possible. The mold consists of a circular base plus inner and outer rings made of metal flashing. You tamp a sand-cement mixture over the bottom and up the sides, wait for the mix to stiffen, and remove the outside ring. Leaving the pot on its base, you can then begin carving.

DIRECTIONS

1 With a jigsaw or a band saw, cut a circular base from ¾-inch-thick plywood or melamine-coated particleboard. For a drain hole, screw through the base into a dowel stub. Cut two lengths of metal flashing to go around the base, plus a little extra. Fit one around the base, tie string to hold the shape, and screw the flashing in place. Tape the overlapped top edge and the outside free end. Form the other piece into a smaller ring. Establish the size by using a thick dowel (about 1¼ inches wide) as a spacer inside the bigger ring. Tie string, then tape the top overlap and the interior free end, and remove the string. Spray the interior with cooking oil.

2 Prepare Basic Sand Mix, page 33, or a bagged sand mix with a minimum amount of water. Pack the mixture into the bottom of the form, then insert the smaller ring and stiffen it by filling the center with bags of sand. Continue filling the form, packing as you go with the same dowel that you used to size the inner ring.

3 After several hours, when the concrete has set, you can begin carving. First, remove screws around the base and cut or peel off tape on the outside ring. You can leave the inner ring in place or remove it by first lifting out the bags of sand. Carve your design using tools similar to those on page 25. If the sand mix is still fairly soft, cut it with a knife. As the concrete hardens, a rasp works better.

The tradition of shaping concrete to resemble wood dates back to at least the 1880s, when French artisans used the technique for garden seats, railings, planters, and trellises that today are considered fine antiques. The craftsmen applied a sand mix to

A faux bois planter

metal mesh or metal armatures and carved the details by hand. Today, you can still make faux bois ("fake wood," in French) this way, but the method shown here is easier. You simply paint a mold material onto actual wood, wait for it to cure, and then peel it off to create a reverse shape that you can use to mold concrete. We used a thick paint-on product sold at pottery-supply companies (see Resources). This material stands up to the alkalinity of cement, so you can cast many duplicates. If you want to make only one or two casts, you can use paint-on latex mold material, which is sold at some crafts and art-supply stores. Mold materials are messy and many create fumes you do not want to breathe. Work outdoors.

DIRECTIONS

1 For a planter, cut a section of a log and brush the bark free of moss and debris. Roll out a piece of potter's clay to make a pad that extends about an inch beyond the end of the log. Push the wider end of the wood into the clay and form the excess clay into a smooth lip. This will shape the top rim of your pot. If your mold material is compatible with petroleum jelly, use it as a mold release. Brush on a thick layer and heat with a hair dryer just until the brush strokes melt and merge.

2 If your mold material is a two-part product, cut disposable plastic drinking cups to about ½-cup size. (It's easier to measure accurately by determining when these cups are full than to fill up to a line.) Wearing gloves, measure the components as specified on the package. Use separate spatulas to scrape the cupfuls into a clear plastic cup. Mix thoroughly with a third spatula. Pour into a fresh plastic cup and stir again. Avoid creating bubbles. Look through the plastic to make sure there are no streaks.

3 With a disposable plastic-bristle brush, coat the greased wood with the mixture. Aim for a thorough coat, not a thick one. While you wait for the mold material to stiffen, wipe off the spatulas so you can reuse them.

Tip

IF YOU HAVE SLABS OF BARK, you can use this technique to cast faux bois steppingstones. They look especially at home in a woodland setting.

4 Prepare a fresh batch of mold material using new plastic cups for mixing containers. Spread over the mold with a spatula. While the material is still soft, smooth short pieces of nylon stocking over the surface and press gently to embed the mesh. The nylon reinforces the mold, protecting against tears.

5 Mix a third batch, again using fresh containers. Coat the surface, paying particular attention to any parts that appear thin. If you see bubbles in the earlier layers, break them and recoat. Put extra mold material around the base so that you have a firm edge.

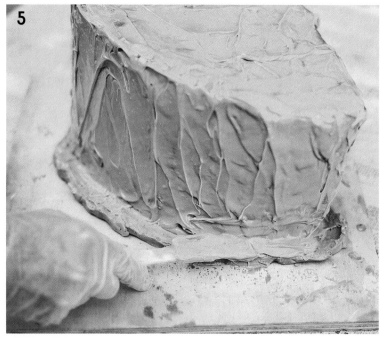

6 The next day, when the mold material is no longer tacky, carefully peel it from the wood as though you were removing a stocking. Turn the mold so that the wood texture faces inward.

7 To complete the mold, find a suitable container to shape the inside surface of your planter. We made one from cardboard and tape and filled it with sand for stiffening. If you are casting a round planter, a yogurt container or similar tub will work well.

8 Prepare Basic Sand Mix, page 33, or a bagged sand mix using concrete bonding adhesive in place of half the water unless the package specifies adding only water. Add pigment, if you wish. Fill the bottom of the mold and jiggle it to settle the mix and raise bubbles. Insert a piece of plastic pipe just long enough to extend through the bottom of the pot to create a drain hole, if desired. Then add the interior mold and finish filling. Tamp as you go, using a stick that fits between the two molds.

9 Create a smooth edge on the finished planter. With a putty knife or another tool, smooth the top edge. To round it slightly cut into the sand mix at an angle along the edges, then smooth the top surface again.

Garden decorations

BELOW: *Two concrete fish add a touch of whimsy to a lovely garden path.*

USING CONCRETE, YOU CAN CREATE MANY DIFFERENT TYPES OF GARDEN ORNAMENTS, including fountains, stands for gazing globes or sundials, and whimsical features that you form in molds you improvise. Keep your eyes open and you'll find clever uses for old rubber gloves, old boots, even old light fixtures. Just remember that molds must either be flexible or they must be free of undercut areas—parts where the mold would be impossible to remove once the concrete hardens. If you use flexible molds, you'll need to support them fully while the concrete stiffens.

132

OPPOSITE, ABOVE: *Simple geometric shapes were combined in an unusual way to create this stunning garden bench.*

ABOVE LEFT: *Because concrete is heavy and rotproof, it makes an ideal base for many garden decorations, such as this sundial.*

ABOVE RIGHT: *You can boost the effect of small concrete features by grouping them. This cherub oversees a water bowl.*

RIGHT: *A tapered pillar of tinted concrete and two pieces of copper pipe soldered together produce an unusual fountain that would be at home in a wide range of gardens.*

This fountain consists of two parts: a back piece molded to the impression left by cattails pressed into potter's clay and a tub adorned with water-lily pads. We cast piping into the back piece, hiding all the tubing, but for an even simpler project you can

A garden fountain

string a hose from the tub through foliage and around the back to the spout. Either way, you won't need any holes in the tub. To keep the back from tipping, bolt it to the tub above the water line. If you have access to a hammer drill and masonry bit, you can drill the bolt holes after you cast the parts. Otherwise, create the necessary holes as you pour the concrete, the method we show here.

DIRECTIONS

1 Buy the pump first so you know how deep your tub must be. Our tub is 24 inches long, 14 inches wide, and 9 inches deep on the outside. Build interior and exterior forms and shape reinforcing, as shown for the sink on page 80, but omit the plumbing details. Notch the base to make a lip that will brace the fountain's back piece.

2 Add a T-brace (sold with builder's hardware) so you can bolt the back to the tub later. Thread 1-inch-long carriage bolts through the two lower holes on the brace and through small holes in the reinforcing cage and add washers and nuts. This allows you to cast the brace into the tub wall.

3 To cast water-lily decorations into the front of the tub, cut shapes from cardboard or foam core and glue them to the mold. We used foam core.

4 Prepare Basic Sand Mix, page 33, or a bagged sand mix. Replace half the mix water with acrylic or latex fortifier. This makes the tub more waterproof. Fill the mold as shown for the sink. First, fill the bottom halfway; then, insert the reinforcing cage and finish filling the bottom. Insert the interior mold and fill the sides. Tap the mold every half-inch or so to work out air gaps. Align the T-brace so that it is flush with the interior of the tub. Fill in behind it, working the mix around the bolts. Smooth the top edge.

5 Cover with plastic and keep damp for several days before removing the forms. To free the interior, remove screws and cut away the foam in layers. A small prybar helps, but don't use it against the concrete.

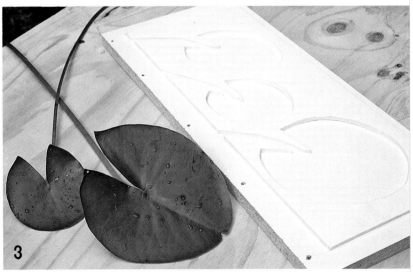

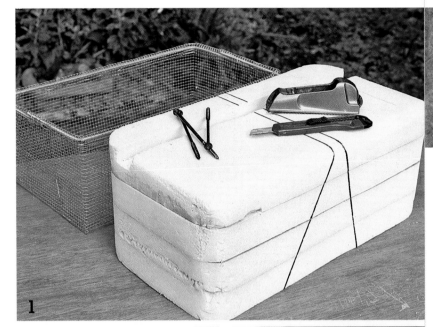

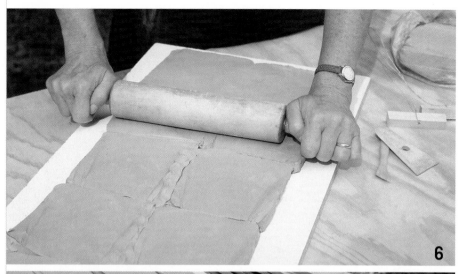

6 Design the back in a size that fits with your tub. Ours is 36 inches tall, 14 inches wide, and 3¼ inches thick. (If you don't cast the piping into the concrete, make it just 2 inches thick.) Cut the form from melamine-coated particleboard. Before you assemble the pieces, slice ½-inch-thick pieces of potter's clay and roll them into a smooth sheet over the bottom of the form. Trim the edges, leaving a gap if you want to create a frame.

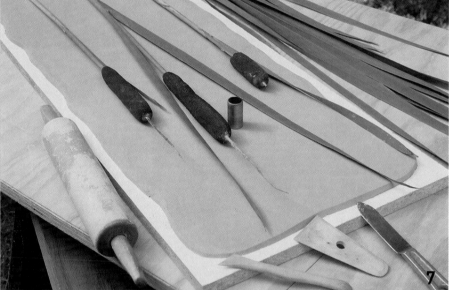

7 Arrange cattails or other suitable decoration on the clay. Use a stub of pipe to stand in for the waterspout so that you can place the other elements around it. The back will sit within the tub, so your design will emerge from the water.

8 Test your decorative materials on a scrap of clay to see whether you must spray them with oil to prevent the clay from sticking. Cattails were fine without it. Press the decorations into the clay. Use a potter's tool or a chopstick where your fingers are too big. Then remove the pieces and spray the clay with cooking oil. If you aren't adding concrete immediately, cover the mold tightly with plastic wrap, then with a plastic bag.

9 Screw the mold together and assemble piping for the fountain. The pump we bought calls for ½-inch tubing, so we used a barbed connector to link a section of underwater tubing with cast-in-place ½-inch CPVC piping. (Standard ½-inch PVC is too thick to hide in concrete this thick.) A couple of 90-degree elbows completed the setup.

10 Using the actual molded tub, make a template from sturdy cardboard or thin plywood to show you exactly where to place the bolt that will connect the back to the T-brace. For reinforcing, cut several pieces of ¼-inch threaded rod 2 inches shorter than the back.

11 Prepare more sand mix. Fill the form using the patty procedure shown on page 70. Take care not to move the piping. When the mold is full, place pencil rods on the surface, spacing them equally starting 1 inch from the sides. Avoid placing rods near the piping. Tamp in, as shown on page 117. Using the template, insert the head end of a bolt with a washer and wiggle the bolt to embed it. Only threads, wrapped with tape, should project from the concrete.

12 Keep damp several days. Remove the mold. Brush and rinse off any stuck clay and fill holes with a paste of cement and water. Highlight raised areas on the backsplash by painting them with diluted latex paint. Bolt on the backsplash. Fill the tub to create an anchor weight.

A garden pedestal makes a good base for a birdbath, gazing globe, sundial, or garden pot. This version has a sculptural look thanks to the way it is built. The main skeleton is a cylindrical form usually used in pouring foundations. Wrapped with hardware cloth

A garden pedestal

and expanded-metal lath, it provides a good base for a cement-and-sand mixture, which glitters in the sun because handfuls of mother-of-pearl were pressed into the surface. The pedestal can support a relatively light load, such as a sundial or globe.

DIRECTIONS

1 First, cut pieces for the skeleton. With a fine-tooth saw, cut a 6-inch-diameter cardboard cylinder 36 inches long. To make a base cone, cut a semicircle of expanded-metal lath. Create the shape by marking two positions as you rotate a stick around a pivot point 28 inches from the end of the sheet. Make one set of marks 9 inches down and the second $27\frac{1}{2}$ inches down. Cut along the two curves with aviator's snips. To wrap the top of the tube, cut one piece of hardware cloth 24 by 24 inches.

2 Using 20-gauge galvanized wire, stitch the lath into a cone and the hardware cloth into a tube. Weave in and out with needle-nose pliers when necessary. Slip the cone and then the tube onto the cardboard and stitch the two metal pieces together. There will be extra hardware cloth at the top. Snip tabs into the excess at the top and fold them in. Stitch with wire.

3 Plaster the form with Basic Sand Mix, page 33, or a bagged sand mix prepared quite stiff. Load the mix onto an inverted trowel, as if it were a mason's hod, and gently push small amounts onto the mesh. Don't attempt to smooth the surface—the next layer sticks better if it's rough. Cover with plastic until the concrete stiffens.

4 Paint the surface with concrete bonding adhesive.

5 Apply the second coat by hand. Pat or trowel it smooth.

6 Add sparkle by pressing mother-of-pearl into the top layer while it is pliable. Dampen the shells first so they don't soak up water from the surrounding cement mix.

Projects from improvised molds

Basically, you can use almost anything that's relatively nonporous as long as it's either stiff or can be fortified to hold heavy concrete without flexing. For the globes shown above, we used old light fixtures as molds. After packing them with a basic sand mix, we inserted dowel stubs in the bases and waited a week before breaking the glass (over a bucket) with a hammer. We drilled matching dowel holes in a post and a rock, and—voilà!—we had garden art. For the mother-of-pearl decoration, smear glue on the inside of the glass and press on the inlays, then add sand mix. The next page shows some of the other ideas that struck our fancy.

SCARECROW

This curious garden guard gets its shape from a variety of found molds plus flexible copper pipe. The face comes from a plastic mask sold at craft stores. A plastic bag set into a bed of sand shaped the rounded back of the head. After the sand mix set, we drilled recesses for the eyes and glued on marbles. We used rubber boots to shape the feet and disposable vinyl gloves, with a wire poked down each finger, for the hands. We inserted a copper coupling into the wet sand mix at the base or top of each mold.

POST HOLDER

An oversize plastic funnel makes a handy mold for an anchor to hold garden ornaments or signs. We glued bits of recycled bottle glass to the inside of the funnel and taped the tip shut. Then we placed the mold (tip side down) in a wide can and filled the funnel with a concrete mix. A few days later, we tipped the concrete out and drilled a matching tapered hole in the post. To create the taper, we used progressively smaller spade bits.

EDGING

To create curb or edging pieces suitable for lining garden beds, paths, and parking areas, we stuck pieces of glazed tile to squares of adhesive shelf paper and placed them in the bottom of a plastic tray sold for wetting sheets of wallpaper. We hooked a couple of clamps over the edges to keep the tray's thin sides from flaring out, then added Basic Concrete Mix and jiggled it to release air bubbles.

DECORATIVE TILE

This lacy tile began as part of a doormat. We sprayed the mat with cooking oil and placed it upside down in the bottom of a box built of melamine-coated particleboard. (A plywood form or one made from cardboard will also work.) Then it's just a matter of adding Basic Concrete Mix or Basic Sand Mix. A tile like this can be used on a path or patio, but it's decorative enough to stand on its own as garden art. Adding a spout will turn it into a backsplash for a garden fountain.

RESOURCES

If you're ready to go ahead with a decorative concrete project, you'll find most of the materials you need at local home-improvement stores. For a wider assortment of pigments, white cement, and special aggregate, look in the phone book under "Concrete—Ready-Mixed." Even though companies listed there most likely sell concrete by the truckload, they usually sell related materials in small quantities or can recommend where to get them. Here's a start on some additional sources of supplies and information; most of the specialty companies ship nationwide.

TECHNICAL INFORMATION

Cast Stone Institute
Lawrenceville, GA
(770) 972-3011
www.caststone.org

Portland Cement Association
Skokie, IL
(847) 966-6200
www.cement.org

ACID STAIN

Colormaker Floors Ltd.
Vancouver, B.C., Canada
(888) 875-9425
www.colormakerfloors.com

Kemiko
Leonard, TX
(903) 587-3708
www.kemiko.com

L. M. Scofield Co.
Douglasville, GA
Los Angeles, CA
(800) 800-9900
www.scofield.com

AGGREGATE

Manufacturers Mineral Co.
Renton, WA
(425) 228-2120

Mesolini Glass Studio
Bainbridge Island, WA
(206) 842-7133
www.mesolini.com

Spectrum Glass Co., Inc.
Woodinville, WA
(425) 483-6699
www.spectrumglass.com

Terrazzo & Stone Supply Co.
Bellevue, WA
(888) 644-5577
Marysville, WA
(877) 534-4477
www.terrazzostone.com

BAGGED MIXES

Buddy Rhodes Concrete Counter Mix
Buddy Rhodes Studio
San Francisco, CA
(877) 706-5303
www.buddyrhodes.com

Quikrete
The Quikrete Companies
Atlanta, GA
(800) 282-5828
www.quikrete.com

Sakrete
Bonsal American
Charlotte, NC
(800) 334-0784
www.bonsal.com

BRASS AND NICKEL GAUGE STRIPS

Terrazzo & Stone Supply Co.
Bellevue, WA
(888) 644-5577
Marysville, WA
(877) 534-4477
www.terrazzostone.com

COLOR HARDENER

L. M. Scofield Co.
Douglasville, GA
Los Angeles, CA
(800) 800-9900
www.scofield.com

CONCRETE: CUSTOM AND READYMADE FOR HOME AND GARDEN

Architectural Concrete Specialties
Phoenix, AZ
(480) 921-3826
www.acsconcrete.com

Art & Maison, Inc.
North Miami, FL
(305) 948-0477
www.artandmaison.com

Artisans Concrete Supply
(360) 509-8651

Buddy Rhodes Studio
San Francisco, CA
(877) 706-5303
www.buddyrhodes.com

Colorado Concrete Concepts
Denver, CO
(720) 374-2101
www.coloradoconcreteconcepts.com

Counter Production
(concrete with recycled glass)
Berkeley, CA
(510) 843-6916
www.counterproduction.com

DEX Studios
Atlanta, GA
(404) 753-0600
www.dexstudios.com

Dogpaw Design
Seattle, WA
(206) 706-0099
www.dogpaw.com

Flying Turtle Cast Concrete
Modesto, CA
(209) 530-1611
www.flyingturtlecastconcrete.com

Form/Function Custom Concrete
Rowley, MA
(978) 432-1093
www.formfunctionconcrete.com

Grotto Designs
Canmore, Alberta, Canada
(866) 262-3966
www.grottodesigns.com

Meld USA
Raleigh, NC
(919) 790-1749
www.meldusa.com

Nichols Bros. Stoneworks
Snohomish, WA
(800) 483-5720
www.nicholsbros.com

Oso Industries
Brooklyn, NY
(347) 365-0389
www.osoindustries.com

R&A Concrete
Arlington, WA
(360) 435-3885
www.raconcrete.com

Robyn Krutch
Bainbridge Island, WA
(206) 842-1121

Sonoma Cast Stone
Sonoma, CA
(888) 807-4234
www.sonomastone.com

Syndesis Inc.
Santa Monica, CA
(310) 829-9932
www.syndesisinc.com

Topher Delaney Studios
San Francisco, CA
(415) 621-9899
www.tdelaney.com

CONTRACTOR LISTINGS
www.concretenetwork.com
www.decorative-concrete.net
www.concreteexchange.com

GARDEN POTS AND SCULPTURE

Nichols Bros. Stoneworks
Snohomish, WA
(800) 483-5720
www.nicholsbros.com

Robyn Krutch
Bainbridge Island, WA
(206) 842-1121

MOLDS

History Stones
Camas, WA
(360) 834-7021
www.historystones.com

PAINT-ON MOLD MATERIAL

Por-A-Mold
Synair Corporation
Chattanooga, TN
(800) 251-7642
www.synair.com

PIGMENTS

Buddy Rhodes Studio
San Francisco, CA
(877) 706-5303
www.buddyrhodes.com

Davis Colors
Beltsville, MD
(800) 638-4444
Los Angeles, CA
(800) 356-4848
www.daviscolors.com

QC Construction Products
Madera, CA
(800) 453-8213
www.qcconprod.com

Solomon Colors
Springfield, IL
(800) 624-0261
www.solomoncolors.com

POLISHING TOOLS

Master Wholesale Inc.
Seattle, WA
(800) 938-7925
www.masterwholesale.com

POLYPROPYLENE FIBERS

Synthetic Industries, Inc.
Chattanooga, TN
(800) 635-2308
www.fibermesh.com

WHITE CEMENT

Butler Enterprises
Post Falls, ID
www.butlerscraftsupplies.com

Lehigh Cement Co.
Allentown, PA
(800) 523-5488
www.lehighwhitecement.com

DESIGN & PHOTOGRAPHY

DESIGN CREDITS

Front Matter

1 David Gibson, The Garden Collection 2 Scogin, Elam + Bray 3 Architect: Gary Garman; concrete features: Buddy Rhodes Studio (www.buddyrhodes.com)

A World of Possibilities

4 Design and construction: David Hertz/Syndesis Inc. (www.syndesisinc.com) 6 top Sonoma Cast Stone (www.sonomastone.com) 6 bottom Geoff Prentiss, Prentiss Architects (www.prentissarch.com) 7 top left Jon Frederick, Dogpaw Design (www.dogpaw.com) 7 top right Bethe Cohen Design Associates (www.bethecohen.com); fireplace construction: DeMattei Construction (www.demattei.com); fireplace: Lennox Hearth Products (www.lennoxhearthproducts.com) 7 lower right Sonoma Cast Stone 7 lower left Buddy Rhodes Studio (www.buddyrhodes.com); architect: Dan Phipps Architects (www.dpaweb.com) 8 top Sonoma Cast Stone 8 bottom Interior design: McDonald & Moore Ltd. (www.mcdonaldmoore.com); countertop construction: Buddy Rhodes Studio (www.buddyrhodes.com) 9 Harland Hand Memorial Garden (www.harlandhandgarden.com) 11 Bathroom design: Dan Phipps Architects (www.dpaweb.com); concrete features: Buddy Rhodes Studio (www.buddyrhodes.com) 12 top Bethe Cohen Design Associates (www.bethecohen.com); fireplace design: Counter Production (www.counterproduction.com); construction: DeMattei Construction (www.demattei.com); fireplace: Lennox Hearth Products (www.lennoxhearthproducts.com) 12 bottom Counter Production (www.counterproduction.com) 15 top Buddy Rhodes Studio (www.buddyrhodes.com) 16 Architect: Frank Stolz, South Coast Architects (www.southcoastarchitects.com); landscape design: Ripley Design Group (www.ripleydesign.com) 17 top and bottom Pat Nordquist, Artisans Concrete Supply 18 Kemiko (www.kemiko.com) 19 top Installer: Jagger Scored/Stained Concrete (www.jaggerssc.com); materials: Kemiko (www.kemiko.com) 22 top History Stones (www.historystonesartisticgardener.com) 22 bottom R.A. Krutch 24 Nichols Bros. Stoneworks (www.nicholsbros.com) 27 Nichols Bros. Stoneworks (www.nicholsbros.com) 38 bottom Kemiko (www.kemiko.com) 39 right Design: Glenn Dugas; table construction: Buddy Rhodes Studio (www.buddyrhodes.com)

Patterns and Styles

40 Ray Iacobacci, Form/Function Custom Concrete (www.formfunctionconcrete.com)

Projects for Your Home and Garden

58 BAR Architects (www.bararch.com) 60 top Architect: Fran Halperin, Halperin and Christ 60 bottom Kiln Works 61 top left Architect: Marion Elliott; countertop construction: Buddy Rhodes Studio (www.buddyrhodes.com) 61 top right Buddy Rhodes Studio (www.buddyrhodes.com) 61 bottom Architect: Lindy Small Architecture 62 top left and middle left Tom Ralston Concrete (www.tomralstonconcrete.com) 62 top right Design: Betsy Brown Ltd. 62 bottom Form/Function Custom Concrete (www.formfunctionconcrete.com) 63 top Ruth Soforenko, Ruth Soforenko Associates; countertop construction: Buddy Rhodes Studio (www.buddyrhodes.com) 63 bottom Eugenia Erskine Jesberg, EJ Interior Design (www.ejinteriordesign.com) 76 middle right and bottom right Sonoma Cast Stone (www.sonomastone.com) 77 Sonoma Cast Stone (www.sonomastone.com) 78 both Sonoma Cast Stone (www.sonomastone.com) 79 top right and top left Sonoma Cast Stone (www.sonomastone.com) 79 bottom Design: Glenn Dugas; construction: Buddy Rhodes Studio (www.buddyrhodes.com) 84 top and bottom Jon Fredericks, Dogpaw Design (www.dogpaw.com) 85 top Sonoma Cast Stone (www.sonomastone.com) 85 bottom Hagy Belzberg Architects (www.belzbergarchitects.com) 86 top left Jon Fredericks, Dogpaw Design (www.dogpaw.com) 86 top right Marion Elliott 86 bottom Jon Fredericks, Dogpaw Design (www.dogpaw.com) 87 top Robinson + Grisaru Architecture (www.rgarch.com) 87 bottom Architect: Tom Bosworth 90 top David Hertz/Syndesis Inc. (www.syndesisinc.com) 90 middle Tom Ralston Concrete 90 bottom Colormaker Floors (www.colormaker.com) 91 top Elliott Elliott Norelius Architecture (elliottelliottnorelius.com) 91 bottom Design: Johnny Grey (www.johnnygrey.com); tile manufacturer: Buddy Rhodes Studio 92 Architect: Karl Wanaselja 93 top left Belinda Benson Interior Design 93 top right, bottom right, and bottom left Colormaker Floors (www.colormaker.com) 94 Rick Cash, R&A Concrete (www.raconcrete.com) 96 middle Design: Kajer Architects (www.kajerarchitects.com); installation: Marshall Barabasch, Patterned Concrete of Southern California (www.patternedconcrete.com) 96 bottom Steve Miller, Concrete Art (www.concreteart.net) 97 bottom Concrete Solutions (www.concretesolutions.com) 98 top Farouk Ramadan, Artistic Gardener (www.historystones.com) 98 bottom Sonoma Cast Stone (www.sonomastone.com) 99 top Design: Topher Delaney (www.tdelaney.com); tiles: Buddy Rhodes Studio 99 bottom Kemiko (www.kemiko.com) 108 top Counter Production (www.counterproduction.com) 108 bottom Buddy Rhodes Studio 109 top left Clodagh Design Studio (www.clodagh.com) 109 top right and bottom David Hertz/Syndesis Inc. (www.syndesisinc.com) 110 top BAR Architects 110 bottom left Rick Cash, R&A Concrete 110 bottom right Cevan Forristt 111 top Betsy Brown Ltd. 111 bottom Mary Norton 119 top right Cindy Jo Rose, Lynn Robinson 119 bottom Carole Vincent, The Garden Collection 132 top Bunny Guinness, The Garden Collection 133 bottom Horiuchi + Solien Landscape Architects (www.horiuchisolien.com)

PHOTO CREDITS

Marion Brenner: 9; Brian Vanden Brink: 2, 87 top, 91 top, 133 bottom; courtesy of Buddy Rhodes Studio: 3 David Duncan Livingston; 7 bottom left John Sutton; 11 Muffy Kibbey; 15 top, 39 right Ken Gutmaker; 61 top left and right David Duncan Livingston; 63 top Sharon Risedorph; 79 bottom Ken Gutmaker; 86 top right David Duncan Livingston; 91 bottom Ken Gutmaker; 108 bottom Ken Gutmaker; courtesy of Colormaker: 90 bottom, 93 top right, bottom left and right; Gary Conaughton: 93 top left, 96 bottom, 97 bottom; courtesy of Counter Production: 12 bottom; courtesy of Davis Colors: 97 top; Liz Eddison: 1, 119 bottom, 132 top; Tria Giovan: 62 top right, 109 top left, 111 top; Jay Graham: 16, 85 top; Jamie Hadley: 7 top right, 12 top, 60 top; Philip Harvey: 96 top; Alex Hayden: 7 top left, 84 both, 86 top left and bottom; courtesy of History Stones: 22 top left, 98 top; James Frederick Housel: 6 bottom; courtesy of Kemiko: 18, 19 both, 38 bottom, 99 bottom; Muffy Kibbey: 8 bottom, 61 bottom, 79 top left, 108 top; Chuck Kuhn: 13, 17 both, 20, 21, 22 right, 23 both, 25 all, 27 top, 28 all, 29 all, 30 both, 31, 32 both, 36, 37 both, 38 top and center, 39 left, 42–57 all, 64–75 all, 80–83 all, 88–89 all, 94–95 all, 100–107 all, 110 bottom left, 112–17 all, 118 top, 120–31 all, 132 bottom, 133 top left, 134–41 all; E. Andrew McKinney: 63 bottom; courtesy of Nichols Bros. Stoneworks: 24, 27 bottom; Marie O'Hara/The Garden Collection: 14 bottom; Bradley Olman: 111 bottom, 118 bottom; Norm Plate: 110 bottom right, 119 top right; Portland Cement Association: 26 top; courtesy of QC Construction: 17 bottom; Eric Roth: 40, 62 bottom; Michael Skott: 87 bottom, 119 top left, 133 top right; J. Scott Smith: 96 center; courtesy of Solomon Colors: 15 bottom; courtesy of Sonoma Cast Stone: 6 top, 7 bottom right, 8 top, 76 center and bottom, 77, 78 both, 79 top right; Tim Street-Porter: 4, 58, 76 top, 85 top, 90 top, 109 top right and bottom, 110 top; John Sutton: 14 top, 60 bottom, 92, 142; courtesy of Tom Ralston Concrete: 62 left top and center, 90 center; courtesy of Topher Delaney Studios: 99 top; David Wakely: 98 bottom; Michael Winokur: 26 center and bottom

INDEX